Y0-EKP-298

THE WORD IS OUT ON
JEFF GORDON

Racing's "answer to Tiger Woods."
—*People*

"Nobody had to teach Michael Jordan how to play basketball, and nobody taught Jeff Gordon how to drive. Both may have been taught the fundamentals, but you don't do what they do unless you're a natural."
—RAY EVERNHAM
Rainbow Warriors crew chief

"Jeff Gordon is smack in the middle of the best ride of his life. He looks a little like Tom Cruise. He gets richer every week. He drives the coolest, fastest car around."
—SCOTT FOWLER
The Charlotte Observer

Books published by The Ballantine Publishing Group
are available at quantity discounts on bulk purchases
for premium, educational, fund-raising, and special
sales use. For details, please call 1-800-733-3000.

NATURAL BORN WINNER

The Jeff Gordon Story

George Mair

BALLANTINE BOOKS • NEW YORK

Sale of this book without a front cover may be unauthorized. If this book is coverless, it may have been reported to the publisher as "unsold or destroyed" and neither the author nor the publisher may have received payment for it.

A Ballantine Book
Published by The Ballantine Publishing Group
Copyright © 1998 by George Mair

This book contains an excerpt from *Wide Open* by Shaun Assael, published by Ballantine Books. Copyright © 1998 by Shaun Assael.

All rights reserved under International and Pan-American Copyright Conventions. Published in the United States by The Ballantine Publishing Group, a division of Random House, Inc., New York, and simultaneously in Canada by Random House of Canada Limited, Toronto.

http://www.randomhouse.com

Library of Congress Catalog Card Number: 97-97155

ISBN 0-345-42419-0

Manufactured in the United States of America

First Edition: March 1998

10 9 8 7 6 5 4 3 2

Contents

Introduction

"This has turned into so much more than I ever anticipated. I have to admit, at my age, you're not expected to do all this. It's amazing to me I've gotten this far."

It's Jeff Gordon talking—the hottest thing in NASCAR racing today. It's amazing that he's amazed because if any athlete was ever born to a sport, it was Jeff. He drove quarter-midgets at five, won the national championship at eight, raced go-karts and beat teenagers at nine, and was a sprint car champion at thirteen—three years before he was old enough to get a driver's license. Of course, this didn't happen by accident. It was planned and guided by Gordon's stepfather, John Bickford, and supported by his mother, Carol. They got Jeff out of bicycles and into the quarter-midget cars when he was four and soon he was racing every weekend somewhere in the United States.

One of the reasons racing was so appealing was the excitement. Jeff, John, and Carol were spending their spare time amid the lights and sights, the sounds and the smells of motor racing and with the emotions of winning and losing. The buzzing of the cars around the track, the inherent danger of an accident, and the carnival atmosphere all made racing fun and stimulating. Jeff, the shy little towheaded kid, was the center of attention and his parents were, too, by reflection. Certainly, they weren't making any money at it. To the contrary, John was investing money all the time from his auto parts business to get the best cars and gear he could afford for Jeff.

All of this was a prelude and overture for what was to come. In a few years, Jeff Gordon would be a name known to stock car racing fans all over the world as the most phenomenal success story in the history of the sport. He would be a multimillionaire married to a beauty queen who would watch alongside the track at every race.

Jeff later reflected on this kaleidoscopic life into which he was thrust: "I think *Sports Illustrated* said it well. They said my life has been a blur ever since I can remember. It all happened so fast."

Darrell Waltrip, a three-time Winston Cup

champ who knows his NASCAR racing, said, "It seems like every ten years a good one comes along, and this is Jeff's cycle. Everybody better do all they can do before he gets any better because I think the show's over."

How this all happened and who helped to create and nurture the Jeff Gordon legend is the story we tell here.

1

Vallejo Beginnings

Jeff Gordon was born in the town of Vallejo located on the eastern reach of San Francisco Bay where the Napa River flows into the bay from the famous Napa Valley wine region. It is a blue-collar industrial town, the home of the Mare Island naval base. Vallejo was founded during the California Gold Rush in 1851 by General Mariano Guadalupe Vallejo.

Jeff Gordon was three months old when his mother, Carol, and father, Will, decided to get a divorce. After the divorce, Jeff and his sister, Kim, lived with their mother.

In 1972, Carol met John Bickford, a man involved in the auto parts business. When Carol and John went out on their first date, it was an omen of their life to come: they went to the races at the Vallejo Speedway with eleven-month-old Jeff and four-year-old Kim tagging along. Three years later, John and

Carol were married. Since many children in their middle-class neighborhood were racing BMX bicycles, they got Jeff one, too—to ride, not race. Carol felt the size difference between her little four-year-old and the much bigger eight-year-olds in the neighborhood was dangerous. "I told John this was not what I wanted to see him do," she said.

John agreed and soon came home with two little cars—a black one for Jeff and a pink one for Kim. Since Carol didn't want the kids racing bikes, they were going to drive quarter-midgets instead. Little Jeff with his helmet and eager expression began racing his quarter-midget with his nickname, "Gordy," painted on the hood. The car was six feet long, powered by a small, one-cylinder engine that developed less than three horsepower. As it turned out, the only accident Jeff had during this phase of his life was when he fell down at his baby-sitter's house and broke his nose.

Soon Jeff and his stepdad clipped the weeds of a nearby fairground and made it into a makeshift track where Jeff practiced. "We'd take that car out every night after I got home from work and run it lap after lap," Bickford said. "Jeff couldn't seem to get enough of it."

This was the sign of what was coming

because Jeff loved the sounds, smells, and feel of racing and his stepfather encouraged him. Years later, Jeff's racing team owner Rick Hendrick summed it up: "Jeff had the talent and John had the vision." John's vision was that of Jeff as a professional race car driver. He saw the spark of excitement and talent that ignited every time his stepson was around racing. John determined that he would nurture that spark into a bright flame. John set the parameters early when he decreed, "If you want to be a professional race car driver, you're going to act like a professional race car driver." It was John's concept that Jeff was going to live, sleep, dress, talk, and eat racing and that's what he did.

They began entering local races. Jeff didn't always win and, worse, had to endure the ridicule of the older kids who drove against him. His first race, as well as the hundreds to follow, was a learning experience with him spinning out at practically every turn. Still, he won often enough to become something of a local prodigy. Jeff Gordon was a damn good driver and the next few years were filled with racing victories and trophies. One home movie the family has shows Jeff driving very aggressively and bullying his way through the pack to speed ahead and win. He clearly was a natural born race driver.

Jeff won his first national championship in 1979, in the quarter-midget division. John carefully coached Jeff and moved him up against better and better competition. John also knew practice, practice, practice was important in honing any skill and he exposed Jeff to as much racing experience as possible. While other young drivers raced twenty weekends a year, Jeff and John were racing every weekend and practicing several times during the week.

In the years that followed, John and Carol Bickford left nothing to accident and nothing was too good for Jeff's budding career. To help pay for this, John sold off Jeff's winning cars at a premium and used the money to buy up to a better machine. Carol did everything a mother could do and more, including driving John and Jeff from track to track while the guys rested along the way. Racing on a track somewhere every weekend was expensive but they did it, even if they had to buy used tires and sleep in the bed of the truck at some racing meets.

Jeff's talent was also confirmed by the fact that older kids in their midteens didn't want to race against him, even when he moved up to ten-horsepower go-karts. When Jeff was nine, he began racing go-karts around Vallejo. He entered twenty-five races and won every one of them against drivers who were six to eight years older. This so irritated the other kids and their families that some parents charged Jeff and John with lying about Jeff's age. His parents had moved Jeff up to go-karts from quarter-midgets to escape the gibes, but it didn't work. They encountered the same sarcastic remarks and the same disbelief at that level, too. So, thinking it might be better, they shifted Jeff up again to superstock light, but it was the same or worse because Jeff was still nine and the opposing drivers were seventeen or older. Jeff wasn't welcome in those racing circles either. John pulled him back for a while to where he raced alternately in both go-kart and quarter-midgets. Jeff won national championships in both classes of cars plus a second quarter-midget championship in 1982. Bickford bragged that they had become the "Penske of the quarter-midgets."

At fourteen, Jeff moved into sprint cars, driving one-thousand-pound cars driven by a seven-hundred-horsepower engine. His sprint car, Number 16, became known and respected throughout the sprint circuit. He was now racing a variety of cars on a variety of circuits. In the next four years, Jeff set a record unmatched by anyone his age—winning twenty-two races, twenty-one poles, and fifty-five top-five finishes. It was the beginning of a long string of championships.

In time, Jeff and John realized they had run out of racing opportunities while based in California. Jeff won practically every trophy there was to win in quarter-midgets and go-karts and couldn't legally drive bigger cars. As Jeff explained, "You're twelve years old and you have been in quarter-midgets for eight years. What's next? I was getting older, not knowing what I wanted to do next."

That was when John Bickford heard about the opportunity in Indiana, the home state of the Indy 500. The appealing part about it was that there were no racing age restrictions. Jeff could drive cars on the track even if he couldn't legally drive on the highway. Jeff later said the authorities probably figured nobody was dumb enough to drive the bigger cars at his age and so they never passed a law forbidding it. The All-Star Series, for example, was a sprint car circuit with no minimum-age rule. So, in 1984, the family moved to Pittsboro, Indiana, twenty-two miles from the Indianapolis 500 track, The Brickyard. John spent $25,000 to put Jeff into a thirteen-hundred-pound sprint car they could also race in the winter season in Florida.

By 1986, Jeff was heavily into sprint car racing. In fact, he had already won three races against some of the best sprint drivers in the territory. In addition to driving at Indiana locations, Jeff and his stepdad were going to Florida tracks and other mid-western tracks. John and Jeff particularly liked the Florida racing, where Jeff was in about twenty-five competitions. The atmosphere in the Southeast, which was much more enthusiastic and supportive toward motor racing than in other parts of the country, made it more enjoyable.

Back in Pittsboro, Jeff attended Tri-West High School, where he did fairly well with his grades. His main focus, however, was expanding his racing experience with an eye on, maybe, qualifying someday for the Indy circuit. As Jeff explained it, "Most of my time was spent racing, so I did miss out on some of the things the other kids did. But I never have regretted it."

Jeff went to school and raced wherever he could. Ironically, he also took driver's education in high school, after having already won more than one hundred races! Todd Osborne was one of Jeff's best friends in high school. He recalled when John Bickford showed up at the motor shop of Todd's father, Lee, and asked him to build a car for Jeff. "Dad thought they were joking," Todd said. "He thought they were nuts. . . . But it worked out."

"I didn't even want to do the car at first because he was so little," Lee said. "But I figured, as long as he didn't sue me, I'd build it."

So they went racing every weekend, with Jeff competing against thirty- and forty-year-old men who raced in sprint cars for a living. Jeff shined in those years as a terrific qualifying race driver, which gave him good pole positions at the beginning of the race. He was still learning how to handle himself in racing competition, but with the guidance of John Bickford, Lee Osborne, and others who saw to it that he had a good car, Jeff was improving all the time. "For being so young, running with good competition on the fast quarter mile, he was doing real well," sprint driver Randy Kinser said. "He'd race as hard as anybody."

Where Jeff was out of control was on go-kart tracks, where he and his pal Todd Osborne would spend downtime. Todd and Jeff spent time at the Osbornes' family vacation place in Michigan and slipped over to nearby Traverse City, which had a lot of go-kart tracks. "We had a pretty good streak going for a couple of summers, getting kicked out of about every go-kart track in the Midwest," Todd said. The two of them would keep racing until the places closed or they had to leave. Then a few days later they would return to school and their driver's education class with instructor Larry Sparks, who said, "I probably didn't teach him a lot as far as driver's ed was concerned."

The boys spent their free time competing against each other, shooting pool, riding skateboards, and playing video racing games. Jeff and Todd went out for the cross-country track team to stay in physical shape. Then they began competing mechanically by building truck engines and their first vehicles—pickup trucks. Jeff's truck is still around: Sparks, the driver's ed teacher, bought it.

Another teacher at Tri-West High who remembers Jeff is Steve Williams. He had not heard of Jeff Gordon when he first moved to Pittsboro, but he was a racing fan and knew about other drivers, such as Darrell Waltrip, Pancho Carter, Lee Osborne, and Mel Larson. That situation soon changed as Jeff began winning races week after week and his local reputation around Tri-West grew. Williams marked Jeff as a normal kid while he was in school but unusual after school when he spent his time racing. On Friday afternoons when school was out, Jeff would disappear from the neighborhood because he was off driving in some race that night. There were times when Jeff would occasionally miss school because of an "illness" that always seemed to occur on a Friday. Williams understood what was going on, and when Monday came and Jeff was back in school, Williams would ask how it had gone at the Eldora or Salem tracks. Williams noted that Jeff would always shrug modestly and say it went okay. In fact, Jeff had often won and sometimes set a track record, but it wasn't his style to flaunt that.

Though he would later move on to the NASCAR capital of Charlotte, North Carolina, Jeff is still a presence around Pittsboro with his face on highway billboards at the city limits announcing "Pittsboro Welcomes You—The Home of Jeff Gordon—NASCAR Driver." Six faculty members at his old high school are card-carrying members of the Jeff Gordon Fan Club, including Williams, who is Number 392. Principal Ron Ward has been offered $50 for his copy of the 1989 school yearbook, with a picture of Jeff as the prom king.

Jeff and Todd squeezed in a lot of teenage activities despite a heavy racing load every Friday, Saturday, and Sunday night—even down to graduation night. "We graduated on a Friday and went to Bloomington Speedway that night to race," Todd said. Jeff was entered in the race and came in fourth.

When high school graduation time came in 1989, Jeff knew he wanted to race cars for a living. He was now in bigger sprint cars sporting 815-horsepower engines and driving open-wheel vehicles on the U.S. Automobile Club circuit. He had already won the USAC championship in full midgets. The question was, where did he go from graduation and sprint cars?

Gordon wound up in stock cars because of his stepfather and mother, who advised him to look into NASCAR. They continued to support him even though John Bickford knew that soon Jeff would have to move into the big leagues and would require hundreds of thousands of dollars—more than the Bickfords could afford. In thinking it over, the Bickfords thought that NASCAR stock racing, which runs vehicles that are enclosed and look much like cars for sale in the average automobile showroom, would make more sense for Jeff. Also, it would be less dangerous—a normal consideration for any parent. Jeff might have liked going into Indy-class racing—which involves a special, open-wheeled vehicle specifically designed for racing—but he was advised that he wasn't old enough to be a part of that world. The

Bickfords convinced Jeff to try a racing school run by famed, old-time stock car driver Buck Baker at his place in Rockingham, North Carolina. Baker was a member of the NASCAR Hall of Fame and he could give Jeff a grown-up taste of NASCAR racing and guide him along if he liked it.

"I knew right away, stock car racing was the way I wanted to go," Jeff said. "The car wasn't like anything I was used to. I loved it."

His mother remembered that day. She said Jeff was nineteen and took a few spins around the Rockingham track in his first stock car and he got so excited that he couldn't wait to get to a phone to call his mother and stepfather. "This is it! This is what I want to do for the rest of my life!" he exclaimed. Carol said to slow down, slow down, but Jeff couldn't because he was so excited and so determined.

It was a wistful time for the Bickfords. They had shepherded their child this far and now they had to let him fly on his own. Jeff was going to move into professional stock car racing, but the family didn't have the big money that it took to take him where he wanted to go, where he was capable of going. So they tried to work out a plan to find him that support during this transition time. They got some help from writer Larry

Nuber, who wrote to his friend Les Richter
in August 1990 asking him to let an up-and-
coming driver out of Pittsboro by the name
of Jeff Gordon into a Busch circuit car on
one of the superspeedways. The Busch circuit is one level of NASCAR racing just
below the top-level Winston Cup circuit.
Nuber touted Jeff as highly experienced with
more than five hundred wins and as a
graduate of several driving schools, including the Buck Baker school. He didn't men-
tion that Jeff had just turned nineteen. Les
Richter approved and Jeff was allowed to
drive at Rockingham, where, incidentally, he
crashed into a car driven by Randy Baker,
the son of the driving school director. By
1991, Jeff had won six hundred races and
eight national titles.

Jeff knew how to take responsibility for
himself. Beyond that, he had the one
common ingredient found in all people who
are notable successes in their endeavors:
persistence. He refused to quit. To Jeff, no
race is finished until he crosses the finish
line, and it doesn't matter what anyone else
does. He was ready for NASCAR. Jeff found
a change from the sprint cars he had been
driving—and it was a difference he liked.
The cars were heavier and handled well,
with good roadability and speed. Jeff felt

comfortable driving them. After Jeff finished the Baker driving school, he moved into the NASCAR Busch National circuit driving for team owner Bill Davis. It was the beginning of a phenomenal professional racing career that would take a giant step forward under surprising circumstances the next year.

Amazingly, Jeff became both 1991 Rookie of the Year in the Busch Grand National circuit and USAC Dirt Track Champion. Many of Jeff's races were televised on ESPN's *Saturday Night Thunder* series, and this began to draw national attention to Jeff even while older drivers were making fun of his youthful appearance, just as they had when he was a young kid.

About this time, a fateful telephone call was made.

The man who got the call described what happened: "I was in New Jersey when Andy Petri called." Petri was calling for a friend who had a young driver who needed a good crew chief to shepherd him along. Petri provided a little more information and the man decided to go and see if this Jeff Gordon was for real. When they met, his first reaction was that the kid looked like he was a fourteen-year-old carrying a briefcase. Later, when Jeff opened his briefcase, the man saw it held a cell phone, a Nintendo game, and a racing magazine, and he thought, What have I gotten into here?

That man was Ray Evernham, and he quickly became Jeff's crew chief, adviser, mentor, and surrogate big brother. They have been together as a winning team ever since.

2

1992—Jeff's NASCAR Year One

Nineteen ninety-two was the year Jeff moved into NASCAR big time and beyond the financial resources of his family. At twenty-one he would become a star in a team supported by the biggest car dealer in America, Rick Hendrick, with over fifty car dealerships around the country and a multimillion-dollar business that made the money for his stable of motor racing teams. The connection between Hendrick and Jeff Gordon happened on a weekend in March when Hendrick accidentally saw an unknown young man driving in a Busch Grand National race in Atlanta against some Winston Cup pros. Although the Busch league was a step beneath the elite Winston Cup circuit, Winston Cup drivers would enter Busch contests to test out tracks that would later be the site of a Winston Cup meet. That was the case one Saturday afternoon when the unknown kid from Indiana was racing against Winston Cup pros Dale Earnhardt and Harry Gant at the moment that Rick Hendrick spotted him.

What Hendrick saw amazed him because Gordon drove wild and loose, not cautiously and tight like most newcomers to the track. Hendrick was sure this crazy young kid was going to spin out because he was pushing his car lap after lap. Hendrick said, "I told a friend who was with me, 'Just watch. In a lap or two that guy's going to bust his fanny. No one can drive a car that's running that loose for long.' "

What they didn't know about this young stranger was that he had already won hundreds of races in his lifetime and never had a serious crash. And this afternoon he was going to add another notch to his record of wins when he took the checkered flag in that three-hundred-mile race at the Atlanta Motor Speedway. Hendrick would remember this young man in the weeks to come.

Jeff added two more victories that season, taking both three-hundred-milers at Charlotte Motor Speedway from the pole. Overall, he won eleven poles—a Grand National single-season record. There seemed no doubt Gordon would graduate to the Winston Cup Series in 1993 with the backing of Davis and

Ford, which had underwritten his entry to NASCAR. But neither Davis nor Ford put their money or their contracts on the table and they continued to let Gordon race for them as essentially a free agent without a contract.

So, in the spring of 1992, while Jeff was driving in the Busch Grand National circuit and attracting a lot of attention, both he and his stepfather were waiting for more than just attention. They wanted a solid offer from a Winston Cup team owner. Rick Hendrick noticed him, but assumed Jeff was under contract to Bill Davis and Ford. Also watching Gordon was the famous Cale Yarborough. He had sent a verbal offer to Gordon through a third party to see if he would be interested in driving Winston Cup for him. Jeff and John Bickford were flattered but cautious and countered with a package deal that included their crew chief, Ray Evernham. Yarborough said no. John Bickford wisely knew Jeff and Ray were a winning team and should stick together.

Meanwhile, Hendrick kept thinking about how Jeff had raced at Atlanta. Then an employee of his told him Jeff didn't have a contract with anybody. Here was one of the hottest novice race drivers on the scene and nobody had shown the sense to sign him to a contract yet! That was when Hendrick moved, and soon he had Jeff Gordon signed to a contract. Hendrick Motorsports provided the financial backing and the team support John Bickford knew his stepson needed. Beyond what Hendrick saw in Jeff as a driver, he saw something much more when he met Jeff in person to negotiate a deal. He saw a team owner's dream! Here was a young man who could not only drive like somebody out of NASCAR heaven, but he was movie-star good-looking, poised without being arrogant, and humble—a word unknown among most veteran drivers. Rick Hendrick had struck gold—pure gold. Beyond that, Hendrick had no problem with Jeff wanting Evernham as crew chief, and the Rainbow Warriors team was born.

This caused some bad feeling at a race in Nazareth, Pennsylvania, when word leaked that Gordon had signed to join Hendrick Motorsports, a Chevrolet operation, in 1993. But the reality was that neither Davis nor Ford officials had protected themselves with a binding contract with Gordon. A lot of "he said's" and "they said's" gushed during the controversy that followed, along with the normal talk of lawsuits, but nothing happened. Gordon and Evernham moved to

Charlotte, North Carolina, to join team owner Rick Hendrick.

It was a stretch for Hendrick's resources at the time because he already had two full-time racing teams. While there was no specific rule about an owner having multiple teams, there was a gentleman's agreement among the owners that no individual would have more than two teams. Hendrick skirted this by listing someone else as an owner of one of the teams. In time, this multiteam issue would heat up because it clearly was the wave of the future in terms of sharing staff and facilities and making money. Gentleman's agreement or not, Hendrick sensed that he had to bring Jeff on board. Meanwhile, Bill Davis, who had planned on starting a Winston Cup team with Gordon as the driver in 1993, instead hired Bobby Labonte to drive his Number 22 car. Now under contract to Hendrick, Jeff continued to race in the Busch National during the rest of 1992, winning eleven poles and three races, which was respectable but did not send anyone's blood racing.

As Jeff Gordon moved to become part of the NASCAR world, he probably wasn't fully aware of the rich, rural American tradition he was becoming a part of—one that reached back to years before he was born.

It began when the Appalachian mountains of the Southeast were filled with small farms and families trying to eke out a living. The women cleaned, washed, and cared for the children while the men worked in the fields, repaired fences, and tended to what little livestock they had. In time, they found a more profitable use of the corn they grew. Back in the woods, alongside hidden springs, they set up distilling units or stills and made corn whiskey they called "moonshine" after the silvery clear look it had in those mason canning jars borrowed from Mama's kitchen.

The problems came when these farmers didn't pay federal tax on their whiskey. Revenue agents—called "revenuers"—came from the city to track them down and put them out of business. That's the reason one might see some farm boy flooring his car down a dirt road with a revenuer or sheriff chasing him trying to arrest him. It would later develop into a rich southern myth about trying to outdrive the revenuers, replete with fireside stories, country songs, oft-told legends, and tales of love, hate, fear, and glory. It would develop into the *Smokey and the Bandit* movies starring Burt Reynolds and, later, TV series such as *The Dukes of Hazzard*. It would have farm boys spending wintry cold nights working on their cars in the barn by lantern light to fine-tune them into racing machines that would leave the sheriff swallowed up in the dust.

Predictably, these same farm boys would gather together from time to time to test themselves and their cars against one another on a stretch of country road or on an improvised oval created in somebody's meadow. From these roots—a deadly cat-and-mouse game between wild moonshine runners and grim old sheriffs on twisting backcounty roads—emerged a purely American sport, stock car racing, and legends named Gober Sosebee, Tim Flock, and Soapy Castles.

By the 1990s, what had started as farm kids tinkering with their cars and racing them now and then and here and there had been transformed into the hottest-growth sport of the era, with heroes like Jeff Gordon, a young man with matinee-idol looks, who would take in $4.3 million in 1995. The sport itself had grown up as well, and even had a fancy name: the National Association of Stock Car Automobile Racing. As times changed, NASCAR racing changed as well, and the days of one man toiling over one car in his barn were replaced by corporate sponsorships.

Now one sees names like DuPont, Kellogg's, Kodak, Tide, Tyson, Goodwrench, and Goodyear as sponsors, with their corporate logos carefully painted on the sides of stock racing cars. Their annual support of the sport amounts to millions of dollars for each car and driver. In fact, present-day racing will see one driver earn thousands of dollars for just a few laps around the racetrack. Oddly, this was bolstered when the federal government banned cigarette advertising from radio and TV and the tobacco companies were left casting about for other ways to keep their names before the public. That motivated tobacco giant R.J. Reynolds to come on board and sponsor the premiere stock car racing competition: the Winston Cup Series. Other businesses followed in time, and the melding of old-time stock car racing with modern corporate marketing resulted in enormous growth for the sport. Today:

- All of the thirty-three races in the Winston Cup Series organized by NASCAR are nationally televised.
- Attendance at the track has skyrocketed, doubling from 2.6 million in 1987 to more than 5 million in 1995.
- A manufacturer of automobile batteries paid $5 million a year so a car could parade its logo around the track at

speeds up to two hundred miles per hour.

- Gross sales in merchandising are approaching the half-billion-dollar mark. For example, "collectibles" ranging in price from $200 racing jackets to $7.95 matched sets of lug nuts swept off the floor of racing great Rusty Wallace's garage.

This was the NASCAR world into which a polite and eager young man from Vallejo, California, and Pittsboro, Indiana, had migrated.

3

1993—Jeff's NASCAR
Year Two

In 1938, a young man finished fifth in the Daytona 500 race, but he would become the future of stock car racing in America. That young man went on to create NASCAR. His name was William France. Fifty-five years later another young man came in fifth in the Daytona 500 and would become the future of stock car racing in America for his generation: Jeff Gordon.

The year 1993 has been called a year full of drama. Names like Dale Earnhardt, Rusty Wallace, Dale Jarrett, and Jeff Gordon kept making the stock car headlines. Sadly, it was also a season when two well-known stock car drivers died, but not on the racetrack. The fans were also making news as more and more of them crowded the speedways to make NASCAR racing one of the most popular sports in the country.

The racing year opened on a positive note during Speedweeks in Daytona Beach, Florida, where the fresh ocean breezes of the Atlantic were called "winds bringing change" for the sport. In an interplay that saw old faces supplanted with new faces there was a symbolic passing of the old era of NASCAR into the modern era of NASCAR. Richard Petty, known as "The King" among the NASCAR set, "passed his steering wheel" and his Number 43 Pontiac to younger driver Rick Wilson. Petty would not be the driver any longer; he would be the team owner. Daytona in 1993 was The King's last race in NASCAR and it was Jeff Gordon's first.

The Daytona 500 is the big NASCAR race of the year and it opens the racing season. Jeff, one of three former Busch Series racing standouts, formed the nucleus of the 1993 rookie class at Daytona. Along with Jeff, Bobby Labonte and Kenny Wallace also made names for themselves, but it was Jeff— and in particular his introductory race at Daytona, the first of the Gatorade Twin 125 races—that left a lasting impression and saw him as number one in Victory Lane. After his first win of the season, Gordon said, "It's unbelievable. . . . If you were on my radio scanner, you would have heard a whole lot of screaming excitement." The rookie dazzled those in the stands and around the racing world.

In the Daytona 500 qualifying heat, Jeff was the youngest driver ever to win. Even so, virtually no one thought Gordon could stand up under the grueling 200 laps at 190 miles per hour in the Daytona 500 and finish in any significant place. But he did.

The race itself was dramatic because it was not settled until the last few laps, when tension, time, and fatigue played a role in deciding who would make the right move at the right moment to win. Three laps from the end, Earnhardt was out in front with Jeff, Jarrett, Bodine, and Hut Stricklin trailing in that order. Jarrett pushed down on the power and pulled by Jeff for second place on the 198th lap. They were all packed in together as they went into the final lap. For most of the last ten laps of the race, Jeff was riding on top of Dale Earnhardt's bumper with only inches between them, both driving at almost two hundred miles an hour. When Jarrett pulled into position alongside Earnhardt, Gordon had a micro-second to decide whether to stick behind Earnhardt or slip in behind Jarrett. He chose wrong and stayed with Earnhardt. One can't predict what will happen in these situations, but it didn't work for Jeff. The power-draft combination of Jarrett-Bodine was more than Earnhardt-Gordon could handle and Jarrett nosed across the finish line just ahead of Earnhardt. In the confusing end, Stricklin was able to maneuver just ahead of Jeff. Jeff finished fifth (but had led the first lap—the first rookie driver in history to do this!).

For many race people, the big part of Jeff's coming to the Daytona Victory Lane that day was his winning the qualifying race, but what made that time memorable to Jeff was not the race or the trophy but the girl who was handing him the trophy. He recognized her as the current Miss Winston, Brooke Sealey, who handed out trophies and kissed the winners on the cheek. Jeff had never met her but knew her from a picture a friend had shown him, commenting that the two of them would be a super match. "I was wowed before I ever met her," Jeff said later. He could hardly even grasp that he had made it to the Daytona 500, won the 125-mile qualifying heat, met the girl of his dreams, and then came in fifth in the Daytona race all in a few days.

Jeff's amazing performance at Daytona brought focus to two things. First, the NASCAR racing world wanted to know more about Jeff Gordon. Second, Jeff realized a rookie's mistake cost him the race: he hesitated at the very moment when it counted. When he had time to reflect, after the race, Jeff said, "This is a whole new ball game. I always lived day to day. I'm still the racer I was five years ago; I've just moved to a big, new level."

He had always been an assertive driver, not shy about making the moves that had to be made, but in this league he was beginning to learn that patience could be his friend. To help him with the right attitude adjustment, he was lucky to have the veteran head of his Rainbow Warriors, crew chief Ray Evernham, who provided a steadying hand. But even Evernham was impressed with the kid driving DuPont Number 24. "I don't think anybody really knows just how talented Jeff Gordon is," Evernham said. "He doesn't even know that."

The Goodwrench 500 followed at the North Carolina Motor Speedway in Rockingham, North Carolina, and then the next race, the Pontiac Excitement 400, at Richmond, Virginia. Gordon was getting the sense of NASCAR and learning the importance of having Ray Evernham as his crew chief with a full, professional crew behind him.

The blizzard of 1993 postponed the Motorcraft 500 at the Atlanta Motor Speedway for a week, but conditions were much improved the following weekend. Again, Jeff would learn a valuable lesson about racing in the Winston Cup circuit when at one point he was in prime position to win the race. However, with just twelve laps to go, Gordon stopped for a "splash of fuel." The stop, which lasted only a few seconds, cost Jeff three positions, and Morgan Shepherd sped ahead to win instead. It underscored the importance of saving fuel, knowing exactly how much fuel you have left, and how critical speed is during pit stops.

The Winston Cup season was edged by tragedy when Alan Kulwicki—the reigning 1992 Winston Cup champion—was one of four victims in a small-plane crash on April 1, 1993. At age thirty-eight, Kulwicki had achieved his lifelong dream—to be a NASCAR champion. He was to have raced a few days later in the Food City 500 at the Bristol International Raceway in Tennessee. Kulwicki's words from his speech at the 1992 NASCAR Awards Banquet haunted those in attendance at Darlington. "There's a lot of guys coming into the sport and maybe some of them will look at [me] and say 'If he can do it, maybe I can do it, too.'" Rusty Wallace won the Food City 500, and he paid tribute to his friend Kulwicki with a clockwise-direction victory lap.

Jeff ran into trouble at the First Union 400 at the North Wilkesboro Speedway, when something went wrong and he crashed into a wall. Given the tragedy of Kulwicki a short time before, everybody was glad that, in spite of a serious fire, Gordon walked away from the wreck—disappointed but unharmed.

At the Sears Point Raceway, near Sonoma, California, 94,000 racing fans watched the Save Mart 300 under the golden California sun. There, Geoff Bodine won his first Winston race of the year. It had a sad side to it since Bodine had just purchased the racing team formerly owned by Alan Kulwicki. The next event in the circuit was the Coca-Cola 600 at the Charlotte Motor Speedway. Dale Earnhardt ultimately won the race, his second of the season, but he said that it was a close one between "many Chevys." Earnhardt gained the checkered flag followed closely by Jeff Gordon, Dale Jarrett, Ken Schrader, and Ernie Irvan. The top five winners made it a "top five" for Chevrolet.

Dover Downs International Speedway, home of the monster mile—one of the most challenging to drive on the Winston Cup circuit—was the site of the Budweiser 500. Familiar names like Wallace, Earnhardt, and Jarrett led the news at Dover Downs, but it was Earnhardt who held off a late charge by

Jarrett to win his second consecutive Winston Cup race—and his third of the season.

Dover took its toll on the men and the cars, and the teams were looking forward to an "easy" race at Pocono International Raceway, site of the Champion Spark Plug 500. It was not to be easy, however. On the fourth lap of the five-hundred-mile race, Rusty Wallace suffered a blown engine, and then Earnhardt developed an oil leak that took him out of contention. Drivers Martin, Irvan, and Bodine also developed engine problems. Kyle Petty, son of The King, racing great Richard Petty, was left to win the race.

The Miller Draft 400, at the Michigan International Speedway, saw Mark Martin build such a commanding lead that he was expected to win the race as easily as Kyle Petty had a few weeks before. But, as is known on the racing circuit, races in Michigan are known to be won on fuel economy. With only nine laps to go, Martin's high-performing vehicle was forced to stop for fuel. This was what Jeff had been forced to do several weeks earlier at Atlanta with a disappointing result. Proving that the fastest car doesn't always win, Ricky Rudd drove his Chevrolet into first place, followed by Jeff Gordon. Both Rudd and Gordon had believed that less horsepower in their cars' engines would result in better fuel economy, and their foresight had helped them in the race.

After fourteen races, midpoint in the Winston Cup Series, Dale Earnhardt was in first place, followed by Dale Jarrett, Rusty Wallace, Kyle Petty, and Morgan Shepherd. Rounding out the top ten were Davey Allison, Ken Schrader, Geoff Bodine, Jimmy Spencer, and young Jeff Gordon. Gordon's tenth-place spot was a surprise; with four top-five finishes he looked assured of Rookie of the Year honors.

The Pepsi 400 at the Daytona International Speedway was won by Dale Earnhardt. The subsequent Slick 50 300 at the newest racing track on the NASCAR circuit, the New Hampshire International Speedway, gave New Englanders their first taste of NASCAR racing. Rusty Wallace triumphed; Davey Allison finished in third place. Less than twenty-four hours after the New Hampshire race, Allison was attempting to land the helicopter he was piloting at Talladega Superspeedway in Alabama. It spun out of control and crashed, killing Allison, who was thirty-two years old. For the second time in four months, the racing world mourned the loss of one of its brightest stars. Allison had made a name for himself both on and off the racetrack.

Subsequent races at Pocono International Speedway (the Miller Draft 500) and Talladega Superspeedway (the Die-Hard 500) were both won by Dale Earnhardt. Races at Watkins Glen (Bud at the Glen), Michigan International Speedway (Champion Spark Plug 400), Bristol International Speedway (Bud 500), and at Darlington Raceway (Mountain Dew Southern 500) were all won by Mark Martin. By the end of August, after some twenty-two races, Dale Earnhardt still led in the standings for the Winston Cup. By November, it was no surprise that Earnhardt would win the Winston Cup championship.

Dale Earnhardt's win capped a year of ups and downs on the circuit. It was a year that saw the death of two NASCAR winners, Alan Kulwicki and Davey Allison. It was also a year that saw the same typical problems indigenous to motor sport racing—problems such as unpredictable weather, pit stops and the problems of rounded lug nuts (preventing the timely changing of tires), engine problems, and auto crashes on the track. On the bright side, younger men were making their names known in NASCAR racing, most notably Jeff Gordon, who would go on to become an even bigger name.

In total, Jeff went through the season being runner-up twice, had five other top-five finishes, and four other top tens. He ended the year with $765,168 in prize money, fourteenth place in the points standings, and being named Rookie of the Year. The one thing Gordon was sorry about was not making it through the season in the top-ten drivers. Offsetting this, however, was his winning a pole at Charlotte toward the end of the season in October, which let him into Daytona's Busch Clash four months later at the beginning of the 1994 season.

By the end of the 1993 season, Jeff Gordon had earned and learned. He made good money and was exposed to some of the fine points of big-time NASCAR driving. In summing it up, he said, "We had a good year. I learned a lot and I had the opportunity to race with the best drivers in the world." It was a promising beginning.

Season number two would be even better.

4

1994—Jeff's NASCAR Year Three

Nineteen ninety-four was going to be more than memorable for Jeff Gordon. Professionally, he came to the new season smarter and more experienced at NASCAR Winston Cup–level racing. Personally, Jeff had already started the year a winner when he announced his engagement to the former Miss Winston beauty queen, Brooke Sealey, whom he met at Daytona in 1993. Everybody agreed Brooke was a positive influence on Jeff. She seemed to calm him and soothe him and, as Jeff said, it made him a better driver.

The new season would be a time of great aspirations, sharp tragedies, and intense emotions for those in NASCAR. It started with an air of excitement as tens of thousands of fans gathered for Speedweeks in Daytona. Informally, Speedweeks begins with the Busch Clash—a contest among the pole winners from the previous year. This is a nonpoints event and serves as a warm-up for the Daytona 500 a week later. Even so, it was a good beginning for Jeff as he started the race in the number six position and drove on to win.

Then, even before the season could get fully under way, tragedy struck. Speedweeks saw the death of Neil Bonnett. While making turn number four of Daytona's course, Bonnett suffered a fatal crash. The tragedy was followed by another fatal crash just three days later when Rodney Oar was killed. Together, the accidents magnified the loss of two of NASCAR's well-known drivers. Fans and drivers alike shared in their grief at the sudden loss. Normal Speedweeks excitement was replaced by sorrow and disbelief.

Jeff expressed the feelings of many when he spoke about the accidents. "Nobody really knows what's going on and why it's happening. . . . They're freak things and nobody likes to see it. . . ." As in any sport, however, the game must go on. And the races did go on at Daytona.

With the memories of both Oar and Bonnett still fresh, race day finally arrived and the Daytona 500 was won by Sterling Marlin. It was a good race for Jeff, too. Starting, just as he had in the earlier Busch

Clash, in the number six position, he finished fourth in the Daytona 500.

Jeff was still looking for his first Winston Cup circuit win after the next race, the Goodwrench 500 at Rockingham, North Carolina. Jeff did well in qualifying for the number three pole position, but problems during the race caused him to finish way back in the pack at thirty-second. In this race, it first seemed Rusty Wallace would have no problem winning his first race of the season, but Sterling Marlin overtook him and Wallace had to work to retake the lead. Wallace came through and crossed the finish line to cheers. His win was his first in a Ford, which is important to all the drivers in NASCAR because of the rivalry between the Ford stock car racers and the Chevy stock car racers and the relative merits of each brand of car.

Jeff Gordon followed with a great race at the Pontiac Excitement 400 on the Richmond track. He began at the number eight pole position and put in a good performance. Then Gordon suffered a misfortune when a few lug nuts were forgotten during a tire change and a wheel fell off his car during lap number 276. The delay cost him valuable time. But his performance had been so good up to that point that, once the wheel was replaced, he still came back to win third place. Over the next several races Victory Lane continued to elude Jeff.

Jeff made a dramatic improvement at the beginning of the Winston Select 500 in Talladega, Alabama, and it looked like he might see his first Winston Cup win of the season. Although starting in fortieth place, Gordon at one point took the lead, but he got caught up in an accident involving a number of cars and ended a disappointing twenty-fourth. Dale Earnhardt, who was having a good year, won his third race of the season.

Then it was out to the West Coast and Northern California's Sonoma County for the Save Mart 300. Jeff did much better at qualifying as he earned the number six starting point only to finish thirty-seventh in the pack. After this race, Jeff's overall Winston Cup point score had dropped him down to eighteenth—which he didn't like. Finally, in Charlotte, everything meshed.

It was the eleventh official race of the season, the Coca-Cola 600, and Jeff was able to hold off challenges from other drivers—most notably Rusty Wallace during the final nine laps—to pick up his first Winston Cup victory on the NASCAR racing circuit. It was an emotional Jeff Gordon who claimed his prize, with tears streaming down his face. It was the rush of thinking how long and hard he had worked to win his first Winston Cup and how many years he had raced to get to this point that welled up inside of him. He described his feelings: "With about ten [laps] to go, I had such a good feeling. . . . We pretty much held the gap on Rusty and I started crying out there in the race car. . . . You can't imagine how hard it is to get to this point. It's just wonderful, it just truly is."

This race also demonstrated how important a smart pit crew is to every driver. Throughout the race, Rusty Wallace and Geoff Bodine dueled for the lead, with Jeff lurking a bit behind in his brilliant, multicolored Number 24 Chevy. With a record crowd watching the first nighttime finish of the classic, Bodine and Wallace pitted for four tires and fuel. Then Jeff came onto the pit road and was out in a flash. Crew chief Ray Evernham had called for only right-side tires, a brilliant decision that put Jeff in the lead. He never gave it up. "That pit stop won the race for us," said Gordon. "It was a great call." It also had a great effect on his overall Winston Cup points ranking, moving him up from eighteenth to thirteenth.

Dover Downs, Delaware, host of the Budweiser 500, was the site of the twelfth NASCAR race, and while Jeff didn't win, he did make a very good showing by coming in fifth after starting way back in the twenty-third spot. Jeff did quite well at the UAW-GM Teamwork 500 at Pocono, starting fourth and crossing the finish line sixth, which put him in the important top-ten finishers and earned him more points. By July, he was still trying to improve his position in the overall scoring. All the while, he was doing well financially, fourth in total winnings behind Ernie Irvan, Dale Earnhardt, and Rusty Wallace.

New Hampshire's Slick 50 300 race opened the second half of the 1994 season—largely notable in that Ricky Rudd not only won his first Winston Cup Series race of 1994, it was also his first victory as both owner and driver. This was another disappointment for Jeff and his Rainbow Warriors team when he ended up way back at thirty-ninth after having started from the number two qualifying position. It was an equipment problem on lap 160—a right rear tire cut down and sent Jeff skidding backward into the wall. Jeff said, "It was really a shame because we had qualified on the outside of the front row and we had a good car under us. That car turned around into the wall so quick, I didn't have any time to react."

The Miller Draft 500, in Long Pond, Penn-

points, but the two kept trading the lead. First Irvan was ahead and Jeff slipped up behind him in his draft to pull air off him and make the lead car looser and more difficult to control. The secret would be for the lead car to break away from the trailing contender and retain control while gaining speed. Then Jeff's strategy changed. He had learned from previous races and now he shifted to a different approach. He realized that he and Ernie could keep trading places and the checkered flag would go to whomever just happened to be ahead at the moment they crossed the finish line. Instead, Gordon decided to use his skill as a driver and pulled up alongside Irvan—but didn't pass him—and stayed there close. His idea was that, by being alongside and crowding Irvan, he might punish Irvan's tires enough so that Jeff would get a chance to shoot ahead at the right moment. Then, with four laps left, Jeff sensed a change in Irvan's driving and knew that he was having tire trouble. He crowded up against Irvan as hard and as close as he could.

Moments later, Irvan's tire went and Gordon shot ahead to the sweetest victory of his racing career. As he circled in the victory lap, everybody from his nearby hometown of Pittsboro was rejoicing, and members of other crews came out of their pits to the edge of the track and cheered Jeff with the victory sign. It was quite a win, and overnight everybody in NASCAR knew the name Jeff Gordon.

Jeff made it a point to take two victory laps to pull himself together so he wouldn't be bawling on TV again, and when he finally stopped and emerged, he was beaming. He admitted he took the extra victory lap so he could get a grip on his emotions and wipe the tears away before he appeared on national television. "I can't control my emotions at a time like this. But I don't want to be known as a crybaby all the time."

Unknown to the fans in the stands and watching on TV, the competition between Gordon and Irvan wasn't the only duel going on in the Brickyard. The Bodine brothers, Geoff and Brett, were having personal troubles. For one thing, their mother was slowly recovering from a heart attack and that worried them both. For another, the two had fought over a souvenir deal and then lost it. Both were going to be out a lot of money. The fight spilled over onto the track as the two began vying for the lead on the ninety-ninth lap, and each took turns bumping the other. In the end, Brett drove his brother into the wall and out of the race. The brotherly attack stunned and deeply hurt the older Geoff. "He spun me out. We've been having some family problems, and he took it out on me on the track. I never expected he'd do it." After the race, when Brett came in second behind Jeff, he lashed back at questioners and obviously had no interest in reconciling with Geoff at that moment. "If there is bad blood, that's personal," he said. "I would not talk about it in public. He's always looking to blame people for something like that. It goes back to when we were kids in his mind. It's not that way in my mind."

Everybody at the Brickyard that day knew that this inaugural race was very important to the future of NASCAR. For Jeff it was personally significant. "That inaugural race was bigger than life. There's only going to be one guy to win the first one. I was that guy. There wasn't anybody in the world that I'd have traded places with at that moment." Jeff didn't even know how much prize money he won until he read about the race in the newspapers. He was $613,000 richer.

The celebration that followed was typically Gordon—he and Brooke were alone in their room at the Speedway Motel watching reruns of the race on TV. A Hendrick Motorsports buddy, Terry Labonte, called to ask what Jeff was doing. He was astonished to learn that Jeff and Brooke were waiting for a pizza to be delivered and watching TV alone. For Gordon, the party was winning the race. There was one extra benefit: at first, the pizza place said it would take almost two hours to deliver a pizza, but when they found out who was calling, they got it there in less than a half hour.

The win was such an important NASCAR moment in history that the Indy officials wanted to buy Jeff's car to put into their motorsports museum. They were told "maybe later" because the Hendrick team planned to race that car again. Another plus from the victory was that Jeff moved up to number eight in the competition for the most Winston Cup points. He now had 2524 points and trailed the leader, Dale Earnhardt, by 581 points.

Following the victory at the Brickyard, some things didn't work out and caused Jeff some problems. Essentially, there were plans for a big celebration back in Pittsboro, his hometown, and Jeff wasn't able to make it, to the disappointment of several hundred fans and friends.

The circumstances were these: Jeff agreed to do a personal appearance at Tri-County Speedway. This is a track located in Haubstadt, where Jeff had often raced while going to high school in Pittsboro. The plan called for Jeff to show up at Tri-County the day after the Brickyard 400 to meet with hundreds of fans and old friends. Unfortunately, Jeff had the luck to win the Brickyard 400; all of a sudden, NASCAR obligations stepped in to ruin the plans. Torn between his promise to his fans on the one hand and his obligation to go along with NASCAR at the beginning of his career on the other hand, Jeff and John Bickford decided he had to do what NASCAR wanted—appear that day at Walt Disney World. A reporter, Bones Bourcier, described the scene at the Tri-State track: "On the afternoon when a few thousand fans converged on tiny little Haubstadt, their hero, Jeff Gordon . . . was riding alongside Mickey Mouse in a theme-park parade a thousand miles away."

The fans were irate and told Jeff so in many calls and letters to newspapers and radio stations. Jeff defended the decision, saying that he knew very well where he came from and where his roots were, but NASCAR felt it very important to capitalize on the win and the Disney World appearance. He said, "It really tears my heart out that we had to miss the fan club meeting following the Brickyard victory." There was also the rumor that he had gone off to play golf on Sunday morning following the race. Not true. He had to do TV interviews set up by NASCAR for whomever won the Brickyard 400. There was a golf tournament going on at the same time, but Jeff wasn't part of it. Jeff assured all his fans that he and Brooke did not go on any rides while in Disney World nor did they get paid any big amount of money—just traveling expenses.

One couple who did show up at the Sunday-morning fan club meeting was John and Carol Bickford. They were there starting at 7 A.M. to apologize that Jeff and Brooke might not be able to join them. John gave everybody the chance to cancel their reservations for the continental breakfast (very few of the 245 there did). Then he did something very savvy, which is indicative of how he has worked for two decades to promote Jeff. John played a recording he made of the two-way radio communications between Jeff driving the last twenty laps of the race and Ray Evernham, his crew chief in the pit. It enabled those at the meeting to relive the final moments before Jeff won.

Next up on the circuit: The Bud at the Glen in Watkins Glen, New York. Jeff started third and ended ninth—in the top ten again. In the next race, the GM Goodwrench Dealer 400, Jeff didn't do as well, starting again at the number three slot, but finishing out of the top ten in number fifteen. Underscoring what a dangerous and fatal year 1994 had been, Ernie Irvan suffered a near-fatal crash during practice sessions at the Michigan International Speedway. While coming through turn number two, where speeds average 170 miles per hour, Irvan's vehicle suffered a punctured tire. The accident forced Irvan's car to plunge violently into the wall, and Irvan had to be airlifted to the hospital. Diagnosed with severe head injuries, Irvan's prognosis for recovery was grim. To the delight of his family and friends, however, Irvan proved the doomsayers wrong and slowly recovered over the weeks that followed.

Other races continued through the season, including the Mountain Dew Southern 500 with Jeff finishing sixth, and the Miller Draft 400, where Jeff came in second.

There were a number of out-of-the-top-ten finishes, too. The competition for the Winston Cup for 1994 was over when Dale Earnhardt won the AC Delco 500 at Rockingham. It was the seventh Winston Cup won by Earnhardt, and it would tie him with The King, Richard Petty, for the most career Winston Cup Series championships.

In spite of it all, in his second big year of

Winston Cup competition, Jeff did remark-
ably well, finishing eighth in the overall Winston Cup point score, which meant he would
be honored for the second consecutive year
at the Winston Cup Annual Awards Banquet
in New York come December. In fact, all
three of the Hendrick teams would be at the
head table. Ken Schrader with the Number
25 Kodak Team finished fourth in the final
scores for the year; Terry Labonte in the
Number 5 Kellogg's car was seventh, and Jeff
Gordon in the Number 24 DuPont car was
eighth.

Jeff, Ken, and Terry weren't the only winners in the Hendrick teams that year. In
October, Ray Evernham was named Crew
Chief of the Year, in recognition of the
immense role of his crew. Ray typically
works the race with Jeff by two-way radio
and they coordinate their strategy. Evernham is also proud that he has the timing
of a Rainbow Warrior pit stop down from
twenty-two seconds to nineteen seconds—
only three seconds, but at 175 miles an hour
out on the track, Jeff can drive a long way in
three seconds.

The only unpleasant thing that happened
during the latter part of the year was the
Ricky Rudd incident. During the race, Jeff
and the crew had trouble with the tires. Jeff's

set didn't come together right and didn't respond the way he wanted them to. As he was going into the race, Gordon was stuck behind Rudd's car, Number 10, and was having a lot of trouble getting around him. "Every move I tried, the Number 10 car blocked," he explained. Jeff didn't have a problem with that because he knows it's a driver's job to protect position and block those trying to get around him. This went on for several laps until Jeff tried to get around Ricky Rudd on a turn. His tires let go and Gordon was afraid there would be trouble, but the tires grabbed and he pulled away. Did the two cars touch? Jeff said if they did, "it was like you might have kissed your algebra teacher." But that wasn't Rudd's reaction. He later told the press that Jeff tried to push him into the wall and do serious damage. Rudd then apparently bumped Jeff three times from the rear. Did Rudd want to make him miserable, pay him back for the earlier contact? The whole incident raised the possibility of NASCAR discipline for one or both drivers, but Gordon just wanted to move on and put it behind him, and NASCAR did not discipline either driver.

By far, the biggest event of the year took place on November twenty-sixth. That day Jeff and Brooke were married at the First

Baptist Church in Charlotte. Ray Evernham was Jeff's best man. The couple took a short honeymoon and then returned so they could go to New York for the Winston Cup Awards Dinner.

At the end of 1994, Jeff could count an amazing assortment of winnings from the year. He was almost $1.8 million richer and had two Winston Cup wins. Perhaps the most lasting trophy of the year—one for life—was his new bride, Brooke. Dale Jarrett succinctly put it in a way that everyone agreed with: "It should be illegal to be that young, that good-looking, and that talented."

Jeff Gordon's successes would prove to be just a prelude to the next year, and 1995 Speedweeks was just a few weeks away.

5

1995—Jeff's NASCAR Year Four

In Jeff Gordon's fourth year of NASCAR racing, the Winston Cup Series began on a high note, even if Jeff's opening race didn't. Nineteen ninety-five would be known as the season in which Jeff would challenge the veteran seven-time Winston Cup champ, Dale Earnhardt. It would also be the season in which Dale's Ford Thunderbird would go head-to-head in competition with Jeff's new, reworked Chevy Monte Carlo—the new stock car replacing Jeff's Chevy Lumina—all as part of the Ford versus Chevy competition.

The 1995 Winston Cup season was under way with the start of the Daytona 500 on February 1. Jeff started strong, but a serious mistake was made during a routine pit stop and he was out of the race. Sterling Marlin won the Daytona 500, for the second year in a row. Marlin became only the third driver to become a back-to-back champ at Daytona.

Ray Evernham, as usual, put the pit problem that eliminated Jeff succinctly: "We just gave the race away. It's just a shame." The incident is a dramatic illustration that no matter how hard and long you practice and fine-tune everything, there is still that element of chance in all human events—particularly in such a split-second sport as motor racing. This is what happened: Jeff had been leading the Daytona 500 for sixty-one laps when he came into the pit. The jack man hoisted up the car, others worked on tires, loaded fuel, cleaned the grille and windshield, all in a few seconds. But the pit man at the left front wheel missed taking off a lug. When the tire changer tried to pull off the worn tire, it wouldn't come loose: the lug nut was still in place. He looked down for his power wrench and, at that very instant, the jack man looked over at him. Seeing a tire on the wheel and the tire man looking away, he assumed the tire had been changed. He triggered the jack and dropped the car down. At that moment Jeff believed the pit stop was successfully completed. He later said, "As soon as I felt the tire go down, I popped the clutch and started out." He didn't get far; he lost the left front tire and sustained some body damage to the left side of the Monte Carlo. The crew tried to repair the damage, but Jeff ended up rolling across the finish line in twenty-second place. Only minutes before, he was headed for a season-opener win.

At Daytona, the business side of racing presented itself when the Frosted Mini-Wheats Division of Kellogg's came on board as sponsor of the Jeff Gordon Fan Club. Among other things, Kellogg's would issue a special cereal box with a picture of Jeff after his Brickyard 400 win on the front. Fans flooded into stores and bought up dozens of boxes at a time, and the initial printing of a million boxes ultimately had to be increased to more than double that. The Jeff Gordon Fan Club was started in 1991 and had forty-seven members, but when Kellogg's came on board, the club roster jumped to six thousand members.

Back on the track, the second race of the 1995 season was the Goodwrench 500 at the Rockingham in Charlotte, North Carolina, and Jeff dominated the event in his new Monte Carlo. The car, prominently displaying the name of Jeff's sponsor, DuPont, was painted in rainbow colors matching the uniforms of Jeff's pit crew, the Rainbow Warriors. Gordon's enthusiasm for the new car was evident after the race. "We just had an awesome car today." He was challenged during the race by Bobby Labonte and Dale Earnhardt. But Gordon outdrove them all and led 239 of 492 laps. Jeff's victory was even sweeter because he started in the number one spot and ended in the number one spot, which gave him a $91,200 bonus from Unocal for a total take that day of over $167,000.

Crew chief Evernham said, "Jeff just doesn't give up." Winning this race took away some of the unhappiness over the Daytona incident the week before. This time the pit stops were flawless as the team followed the strategy Ray and Jeff had worked out, which included changing only two tires instead of all four. Evernham answered his critics by explaining that Jeff had only eleven laps on his tires from the previous pit stop, and by only changing two tires and putting him back on the track in a hurry, they could pick up extra points for the number of laps Jeff was leading. That was just how it worked out.

Problems returned on March 5 at the Pontiac Excitement 400, at the Richmond International Speedway. Jeff's new Monte Carlo was having trouble functioning as well as it should. In the Pontiac Excitement, the fuel pump went out and Jeff was able to complete just sixty laps. It wasn't all bad for the

Hendrick teams because teammate Terry Labonte crossed the finish line first in his "Kellogg's Machine." Even so, that didn't satisfy Jeff, Ray, or the Rainbow Warriors, for whom number one is the only acceptable finishing position. Things were looking much better a week later with a checkered flag finish in the Purolator 500 at the Atlanta Motor Speedway. This time Gordon was drawing incredible speeds, so that, at one point in the race, he was seventeen seconds ahead of everyone else—a huge lead at the speeds NASCAR cars travel. After winning the race and happily cruising to the Victory Lane, Gordon admitted that Bobby Labonte was pressing him pretty hard toward the end of the race. "Bobby got me pretty nervous at the end of the race." Even so, Jeff won and was talking about how pleased he was with the car they were now using. Then it was on to Darlington and the TranSouth Financial 400.

"The Track Too Tough to Tame"—the nickname turned out to ring true for Jeff. One positive part of the day was the tentative return of Ernie Irvan for the first time since his wreck at the Michigan Speedway seven months earlier. Irvan wasn't in the race, but he tested a stock car in some of the trials.

Jeff started out well and it looked like it

could be another winning day with his leading 100 of the first 190 laps of the race, but it was not to be. Randy LaJoie spun his car and came around right in front of Jeff. Jeff couldn't avoid slamming into him. "I don't know what happened. . . ." said Jeff. "I just saw LaJoie spin right in front of me. . . . It was like, 'Where am I gonna go?'" Jeff tried to maneuver around the mess, but there was no room on either side and that was the end of the race for him. He finished in the thirty-sixth spot after a superb qualifying race the day before, running at over 170 miles per hour and pulling the number one starting spot. The TranSouth Financial 400 went to Sterling Marlin in his Chevy Monte Carlo.

By April, the season had been uneven for Jeff even though he had four poles and three wins out of the first seven races, and was the only driver to lead a lap in every race in the season so far. Things picked up when he finished first at Rockingham, Hampton, and Bristol. After that, the action moved to the First Union 400 at North Wilkesboro in North Carolina, where he took on Dale Earnhardt, nicknamed The Black Knight, and managed to snare second place behind Earnhardt, who won with a comfortable thirteen-second margin.

The Winston Cup circuit moved on to the Hanes 500 at the Virginia Speedway in Martinsville, where the Fords finally made a showing at the finish line. Rusty Wallace, driving a Ford, won and Jeff finished a very respectable third. Fords did it again the following week at the Winston Select 500 running on the Talladega Speedway, with Mark Martin driving to his first win of the year. Again Jeff performed well, finishing the race just behind Martin in the second spot.

At this point, nine races into the Winston Cup circuit's 1995 season, Jeff and Dale Earnhardt were tied in the points scores, with each having 1314 points toward the championship. Dale Earnhardt would go on to win the next race, the Save Mart Supermarkets 300 in Sonoma County, while Jeff landed in the number three spot. All these finishes in the top five or the top ten added points in the competition for the Winston Cup at the end of the season. They were adding up.

After Chevys won eight of the first ten races of the 1995 season, NASCAR determined that it was time for a few changes. As a result of tests run earlier in the season, NASCAR reduced the size of the rear spoilers on the Chevy Monte Carlo and raised the rear spoilers on the Fords and

Pontiacs. Raising the spoilers resulted in more downward wind force because of the way the wind turbulence swirls around the finlike spoilers. The more downward wind force means the more downward pressure on the rear tires and the more traction and greater thrust the car develops. The Chevy teams didn't like it, but didn't say anything at the time and just tried to deal with the new arrangement.

Meanwhile, Jeff would dominate the Winston Select at Charlotte Motor Speedway— NASCAR's all-star race. It was all Gordon during all three segments of the Winston Select, and because he won all three segments of the race, he was the winner of a $300,000 prize bonus. The Winston Select was a nonpoints race, but it was still a good feeling for Jeff to finish first and to earn the bonus.

He wasn't so lucky the following week at the same track. Jeff was the favorite at the Coca-Cola 600 and the pole-setter. But he lost a wheel on lap seventy-eight and was forced to sit out the rest of the race. Still, at this point, the 1995 season wasn't going too badly. Even with the uneven luck he and his team had encountered, Jeff had earned seven poles, three regular race wins, and was the top money winner so far. Then came some more bad luck.

Other teams manipulated their equipment and cars to squeeze out every racing advantage possible—and NASCAR inspectors cited them for it. The teams were caught with illegal parts and subsequently fined: the Bill Davis team had to pay a $25,000 fine for an illegal trunk-lowering device; Junior Johnson had to pay $35,000 for an illegal manifold; and Ricky Rudd was fined $50,000 for another trunk-lowering device. Now it was the Rainbow Warriors' turn. They were cited for using an unapproved part—not an illegal one—on Jeff's car and they immediately accepted the blame for the mistake. The part was a hub bought off the shelf from a recognized motor racing dealer, but the team was fined for using it. So Ray Evernham paid a record-high $60,000 to NASCAR for an unapproved, potentially dangerous hubcap on Gordon's Monte Carlo.

Kyle Petty won the next NASCAR race, the Miller Genuine Draft 500 at Dover Downs. It was Petty's first NASCAR win in two years, and even more momentous given the fact that he started the race in thirty-seventh place. Jeff started in the number one pole position, but ended sixth—still getting points for being one of the top-ten winners. The

NASCAR point system was helping Jeff because, while he didn't finish first all the time,
he was in the top-five or top-ten finishers a
good deal of the time and this kept him accu-
mulating Winston Cup points. The brothers
Labonte shared victories at the next two races:
Terry Labonte at the UAW-GM Teamwork 500
at the Pocono Raceway; brother Bobby at the
Miller Genuine Draft 400 at the Michigan
International Speedway.

Jeff, still in first place in the points standings for the Winston Cup, would come back
to win the next two races. At the Pepsi 400 at
Daytona, Gordon attributed the win largely
to his team. "You know, we had a great pit
stop. We lost this thing in the pits in February, but they won this one for us in the
pits." In this case, the pit crew got Jeff back
on the track fast enough to hold off Earnhardt and Sterling. To use Jeff's favorite
adjective, it was "awesome." And so was
the next race, when Gordon would try to
become the first driver of the 1995 season to
win back-to-back NASCAR races. At the
Slick 50 300 at New Hampshire International Speedway, he not only won the race
but also got a $50,000 bonus from Gatorade
for leading the points halfway through the
season. A mark of his skill was that Jeff won

the Slick 50 300 after starting from twenty-first place.

The Miller Genuine Draft 500 at Pocono was won by Dale Jarrett; Jeff came in second. The next week at the Die-Hard 500 on the Talladega track in Alabama he finished eighth with Sterling Marlin the winner. In both races, Jeff picked up points for top-five or top-ten finishes.

Back in Indianapolis, the site of his inaugural Brickyard triumph, Jeff set a new pole qualifying record of 172.536 mph at the second running of the Brickyard 400. There was a scary moment in the qualifying race when the back end of his car broke loose going into the final turn. Jeff said he felt he was heading into a wall crash and he eased off the gas a little, which enabled him to maintain control and finish in first place. In the race itself he finished sixth, with Dale Earnhardt getting the winning checkered flag.

The next three races of the season all ended with top-ten finishes for Jeff Gordon. At one of them, however, Jeff was involved in an incident involving Kenny Schrader and said it was the worst thing in his racing career. He said he realized what was happening when he watched his rearview mirror in horror as Kenny was flipping through the air. Apparently, Jeff passed Kenny, believing he had enough room. Instead he touched him a few inches going at those high speeds and that turned Kenny's car enough for Ricky Craven to clip under him and send Ricky and his Number 41 Budweiser car spinning. Jeff was sick about the incident and relieved when Kenny made it to the pit. Jeff heard on the radio that Kenny was okay.

Gordon showed patience throughout the next race, the Mountain Dew Southern 500 at Darlington. After inadvertently initiating an accident that in turn caused numerous cars to crash (but escaping relatively unscathed himself), Jeff went on to survive late-race challenges by Dale Jarrett, Dale Earnhardt, and Rusty Wallace. The win marked a big step toward achieving the Winston Cup, and Jeff again credited his team: "I tell you, this team was championship caliber today, that's for sure." Jeff felt he had been in a tough battle with Earnhardt and Wallace throughout the entire race and that the efficient pit stops kept him on the track in the best condition and that was the winning edge.

It was all Jeff Gordon two races later at the MBNA 500 at Dover Downs. Gordon dominated most of the race by leading four hundred of five hundred laps before winning his seventh race of the season.

Ernie Irvan marked his return to the NASCAR Winston Cup circuit by taking the lead at one point during the Tyson Holly Farms 400 in North Wilkesboro, and then ultimately finishing in sixth place. It was a strong finish for a man many thought would never race again, let alone survive an accident that nearly killed him, and Jeff was among the many drivers glad to see Irvan back behind the wheel.

With only four races left in the 1995 season, it looked to be a battle between Dale Earnhardt and Jeff Gordon. After the North Wilkesboro race, Jeff was leading in points for the Winston Cup, 4201 to 3899, and he had seven wins for the season to Dale's four. Still, it was close and a lot of things could happen. The next two races proved that point.

Mark Martin won the UAW-GM Quality 500 at Charlotte. While Jeff started in a solid number three position, mechanical problems continued to haunt the Rainbow Warriors. Later Jeff would say, "We took a hard hit at Charlotte. . . . We broke a ring gear in the rear end, one of those things that just does not happen—but it did." Jeff thought it proved you have to earn everything, put your faith in God, and work as hard as you can. Then came the AC-Delco 400 at Rockingham and another disappointment: Ward Burton won, Earnhardt finished seventh, and Gordon trailed in a disappointing twentieth place.

Jeff came out of Rockingham and said that the competition for the Winston Cup had come down to the last two races of the season, the Slick 50 500 in Phoenix and the final race of the year, the NAPA 500 in Hampton, Georgia. He said the Rainbow Warriors were in shape for a strong finish and he was confident they would make it, but the races still had to be run and luck was still a major factor, as it had been all season. Ricky Rudd won the Slick 50 500. Close behind him were Dale Earnhardt in third place and Jeff in fifth place. Jeff Gordon seemed to have the 1995 Winston Cup sewn up—he needed only to finish no worse than forty-first place, but if, for any reason, he didn't finish the race, he would give Dale Earnhardt his eighth Winston Cup.

The final race of the 1995 season arrived on November 12. Apprehension was in the air at the NAPA 500 in Georgia. Earnhardt wound up winning the NAPA 500—he led 268 of 328 laps, but it didn't matter: Jeff finished thirty-second, fourteen laps down, and still won *his first Winston Cup*! For Jeff Gordon this was an extraordinary achievement. At age twenty-four, he had reached the highest goal attainable. It was, again, an emotional win for Gordon. He said, "The Winston Cup championship is just the ultimate thing, and now here I am achieving that. It's just too good to be true."

To some it is curious that he should finish thirty-second in this final race and still garner the Winston Cup. This is because of all the points he had steadily earned over the year in the prior thirty official races. It showed he was a consistent driver backed by a superior crew. Often his poor showings in a race were due to mechanical failure, but those were rare. In a season of thirty-one races, Jeff won seven, finished among the top five in nineteen, plus finished in the top ten in six more. In total, out of thirty-one races, he won or finished in the top ten in twenty-five of them. Jeff's earnings in 1995 were over $4.3 million.

Gordon became the second-youngest driver ever to win the coveted Winston Cup, and with his win he achieved a new level of respect among his peers. He would still be known as "The Kid," yet despite his youthfulness he was a champ. He did it in only his third year as a NASCAR driver. As he had throughout the season, however, Gordon credited his team for his success. His Rainbow Warriors were the key. Through crashes, NASCAR fines, and car-handling problems, he said, "They just wouldn't give up."

6

1996—Jeff's NASCAR Year Five

Jeff, who ran cross-country track in high school, still keeps physically sharp for the demands of motor racing. He was in prime condition starting the 1996 season. He was ready.

His fans, however, were fretting over Ray Evernham's assuming responsibility for racing car Number 25 in addition to Jeff's Number 24. They weren't sure Ray would be devoting enough attention to Jeff. So at the beginning of the year, Jeff reassured everyone that Ray could handle both cars with no trouble.

This was a year in which three Winston Cup drivers contended for the top spot throughout much of the season. Jeff Gordon would dominate the points standings with a whopping ten Winston Cup race wins, but he would battle for the top spot with Terry Labonte and Dale Earnhardt through most of the year. Nineteen ninety-six also saw the typical crashes and pileups associated with stock car racing, and there were emotional moments as well—the racing circuit would say good-bye to an old friend: North Wilkes-boro Speedway would host its last NASCAR race. But first, the season was set to begin at Daytona, and men like Dale Earnhardt, Ernie Irvan, Dale Jarrett, Jeff Gordon, and thirty-nine other drivers wanted to see themselves in Victory Lane at the conclusion of NASCAR's biggest race.

Jeff had problems early in the race when, on lap number nine, he was bumped from behind by Jeremy Mayfield and sent crashing into the wall on turn four. Although Gordon tried to straighten his car out and prevent the crash, his action was futile as the accident happened at a spot on the track known as the "tunnel bump," a slight hump in the racetrack that is located over the two-way tunnel leading in and out of Daytona International Speedway's infield. A chain reaction was thus set in motion that would claim six cars and set out the first caution flag of the day.

Gordon recalled, "I got to the outside of [Jeremy] Mayfield going into turn three. . . . I was up against the wall as far as I could get to make sure we didn't touch. I had a feeling something was going to happen, and it did." With that he crashed and his car was out of the race until the crew could repair it, so Gordon took Brooke's hand and walked to their motor home to watch the race on television. The Rainbow Warriors with Ray Evernham tried to put Gordon's Number 24 Monte Carlo back together in time to at least finish the race. Nearly two hours later, the engine was fired up. Blue smoke poured from the car upon early ignition, but the Monte Carlo soon settled into a comfortable running purr. Gordon was called, and he arrived within a minute—still in his uniform and ready to go.

Once Gordon eased his stock car back onto the speedway, he found himself down by 105 laps; the leader, Bill Elliott, was on lap 116 of 200. Then Gordon started having steering problems and reported to Evernham, "It's slow, it's pulling."

"Better bring it on in, then. We don't want to do any more damage," radioed Evernham.

So Gordon, 1995's Winston Cup champ, was finished for the day. He would wind up with a forty-second-place finish, but he was upbeat when he spoke to reporters before departing: "We've got a strong team. . . . We'll be ready for Rockingham." He would hear on the radio later that afternoon that he had officially completed thirteen laps and won $59,052.

Gordon's payoff eclipsed that of other drivers such as Davey Martin. Martin wound up completing the race, placing fifteenth overall, but would take home $7,000 less than Gordon. This was due, in large part, to a bonus system that dates back three decades under which NASCAR rewards its stars with "appearance" money. This reward system is an outgrowth of a rule from the late 1940s in which new tracks (some of them struggling to attract spectators) would pay a big-name driver just to show up for the race.

Today's system of rewards is based upon the previous year's final points standings. In effect, the field of more than forty drivers is divided into three categories according to the previous year's final standings: the top ten, the middle of the pack, and the also-rans. In 1995, Jeff had won the Winston Cup partially because he was regularly in the first group, the top ten. At the beginning of the subsequent season a higher number is assigned to the most successful drivers, which gives them an edge over other drivers and encourages them to come back to race another year to please the fans. So, for example, a lap led by Gordon, 1995's defend-

ing champion in 1996, would be worth far
more than a lap led by Martin.

Jeff Gordon suffered more problems
during NASCAR's second race of the season,
the Goodwrench 400 at Rockingham's North
Carolina Motor Speedway. Gordon's engine
expired early in the race, and he had to settle
for finishing in fortieth place. Dale Earnhardt propelled himself to an easy victory.
So February didn't turn out well for the
Rainbow Warriors and some fans said it was
because Ray Evernham was handling two
teams—car Number 24 and car Number
25—and not giving proper attention to Jeff.

Finally things began to happen right at the
Pontiac Excitement 400 at Richmond when
Jeff won his first victory of 1996. He reflected: "We needed this so bad. It's been a
tough couple of races. . . ." He was particularly concerned about the morale among the
Rainbow Warriors. He knew they did a superior job for him, but all sorts of things happened and Jeff wanted Ray and all the
Warriors to know that he appreciated the job
they were all working so hard to do. The win
was a combination of Jeff's skill and Ray's
clever tactics. In this instance, Evernham
adjusted the tire pressure on Jeff's car when
it came in for the final pit stop of the day.
Jeff pulled out of the pit quickly into first

position, which he held until the checkered flag. Then, at Hampton, Georgia, for the Purolator 500, Jeff ended in the number three spot after starting buried in the pack at number twenty-one. The year was beginning to look better. Dale Earnhardt was also looking good, with a win at the Purolator 500 making him the Atlanta Motor Speedway's all-time career winner.

Everybody was still trying to tame the track at Darlington International Raceway. Dale Jarrett and Jeff Gordon battled for the top spot of the TranSouth 400 and Jeff wound up winning the race—his second win in three races. Jeff jumped from twenty-third place in the NASCAR Winston Cup points standings to ninth place in just two weeks.

Rain delayed the Food City 500 at Bristol Motor Speedway in Tennessee, but once the race got under way, Jeff lead at lap 107. The race was close when a red flag called a halt. The heavy rain continued to make the track unsafe. The Evernham crew had made Jeff's pit stop super fast. Not seeing a stop signal on the line of pits, Ray told Jeff to get out on the track and let the NASCAR officials make the decision about who was the winner. Gordon was declared the winner by virtue of his being in the lead. Later he exclaimed, "I can't believe we just won at Bristol this way—this is amazing!" It isn't just steering a car that wins races; it is also having the track smarts about what to do and when to do it.

With this win, things were looking better and Gordon's fans were now dismissing the first two races of the year, Daytona and Rockingham, as write-off mistakes and were focusing on the four races that followed those opening two disasters. In the last four races, Jeff was in the Victory Lane three times. He won at Richmond, Darlington, and Bristol, which some observers began calling a fairy-tale turnaround. Jeff came up from the bottom of the barrel in Winston Cup circuit points to number six and was climbing. This was just about where he was in 1995 when he ended up national champion. Commenting on the year so far (six races out of thirty-one to be run), Jeff said, "It was a bummer of a start, but hopefully we are back on track."

On April 14, everybody was back on track running the First Union 400 at North Wilkesboro Speedway. It was a memorable day for Terry Labonte in that it marked his 513th consecutive Winston Cup start, a number that tied him with Richard "The King" Petty for the most consecutive starts. Labonte also completed his day in style, just beating out Jeff Gordon. Rusty Wallace won the next

Winston Cup race, the Goody's 500 at Martinsville Speedway. The win was Wallace's first of 1996, and close behind him were Ernie Irvan in second place and Jeff Gordon in third. Jeff's strong finish marked his sixth straight top-three finish, earning him important points each time.

Prior to the start of the next racing weekend in Talladega, Alabama, NASCAR decreed that three stock cars would be tested to compare horsepower numbers: one Ford was selected (from Ernie Irvan's camp), one Chevy (belonging to Sterling Marlin), and one Pontiac (belonging to Bobby Hamilton). The cars were selected randomly from each camp, and NASCAR defended its decision by issuing a statement: "Our goals and our intentions are, number one, to make the sport safer . . . and make it better for the fans. Close competition is number two on our list." There was growing competition between the teams racing Fords and Chevrolets, like Jeff's Monte Carlo. Crew chief Evernham carefully watched what the NASCAR officials were doing because he felt Fords were getting an unfair edge. Still, he didn't say anything publicly about it yet.

Sterling Marlin wound up winning the Winston Select 500 at Talladega, but an accident in which Jeff and Mark Martin touched each other's car set off a chain reaction that soon involved fourteen autos. Jeff said later that he knew it would be a mess and closed his eyes hoping for the best, but every time he opened them there were car parts flying all over the landscape. He finished in the thirty-third position. The accident showed that NASCAR's safety rules worked. Ricky Craven's Chevrolet Monte Carlo was traveling upward of 190 miles per hour when he was caught in the pileup. His car was devastated—carburetor sheared away, engine pushed completely to the left, and auto body totally crumpled. Yet Craven was able to walk away from the accident. His roll-cage remained intact, his cockpit stayed together as did the fuel cell (so there was no fire), and his special seat absorbed the energy of the crash. Although Craven left the incident unmarked, his wife was so upset about the crash that she gave Craven a black eye herself!

At the Save Mart 300 on May 5 in Sonoma, Jeff said the crew kept working the car at every stop to get it in and out in the best position. At the first pit stop, Jeff came in from the sixth position and the crew was able to get him back out in the fourth position. They repeated that on the next stop and Jeff found himself in second out of the pit.

Then in the final laps a caution flag came on and when Jeff restarted, he spun his wheels and slipped to sixth place at the finish. That depressed him because he felt he could have won the race. Jeff was unhappy because the pit crew had worked hard to improve his position in the race and he lost that by a miscue in getting back on the track.

Rusty Wallace would win the day, marking his first road course win in five years. Unfortunately, Wallace was fined $25,000 the same day because his car did not reach the minimum height requirements set by NASCAR. But since it was only three-sixteenths of an inch short, NASCAR also determined that it wasn't an "enhancement," and he was allowed to keep his win.

Three weeks later, Jeff came in fourth at the Coca-Cola 600. The next two races were much better with back-to-back wins for Jeff and the Rainbow Warrior team at the Dover 500 in Dover, Delaware, and the UAW-GM Teamwork 500 at Long Pond, Pennsylvania.

The Miller 400 marked the midpoint of the season, and the competition for the Winston Cup found Dale Earnhardt, Terry Labonte, and Jeff Gordon in first, second, and third place, respectively. Earnhardt had 1968 points, Terry Labonte 1916, and Jeff 1904.

Speaking of Numbers

Car numbers are curious in that they often take on a special identity with the driver and team, and sometimes become the source of controversy. For fans, their favorite driver's number becomes a lucky charm. For example, here are the official, state-issued license plates some of Jeff's fans have for good luck.

Henrietta Jenkins of Tennessee	24 WINS
Tina Collins of West Virginia	24 FAN
Ken Charleston of Arkansas	GRDN 24
Kodi Gomez of California	DUPNT 24
Monty Browning of Virginia	24-JGRCN
Dave and Cheryl Baxter of Indiana	C 24 GO
Marilyn Bauer of Virginia (Number 3 is Dale Earnhardt)	3OUT-24n
Edward Kronmeister of Virginia (WC is Winston Cup)	WC 24 FN
Jodi Winkle of Tennessee	IM4 24
Michele Cone of New Hampshire	24 JFGN
Donna Peck of Maryland	24 RULZ

When the team of Harry Melling and Bill Elliott broke up, everything was settled amicably until they got to the number. Each man felt it was *his* number and his personal property. In the end, it was determined that the number belonged to the team owner, Harry Melling, and he told Bill it was not for sale at any price.

NASCAR does not assign the numbers but grants them in response to requests by a team. Roger Penske, for example, is a team owner obsessed with single-digit numbers. Rick Hendrick's original designation was Five Star and all his cars had numbers ending in 5—including car 5, car 25, and car 35. Some people expected 35 would be the number for Jeff Gordon's car when he started with Hendrick. Instead, they almost picked 46 because that was the number of the car Tom Cruise drove in the movie *Days of Thunder*, and Hendrick had supplied the car that Cruise drove.

Bobby Allison always liked the number 2 and he has had cars numbered 2, 12, and 22, but always seems to come back to 12. Another owner of 22 at one time was Burt Reynolds because that was the number on his football jersey in college.

Jeff has had the numbers 4 and 6 recur in his career and for the first sixteen years of his racing life, 16 was his number. Some think his present car number—Number 24—stems from his home address when he lived in Pittsboro. That was 6246.

July 6 found Jeff back at Daytona International Speedway, where he had started the year so poorly. The Pepsi 400 was delayed for three hours due to rain, but Gordon's pole position enabled him to start the race on a high note. Sterling Marlin went on to win with Jeff coming in third. The next two races didn't go well for Jeff, again with a thirty-fourth-place finish at the Slick 50 300 in Loudon, New Hampshire. The winner was Ernie Irvan, who won his first NASCAR race in almost a year since he was so terribly injured. A week later Jeff finished seventh at the Miller 500 at Long Pond, Pennsylvania.

A rain delay of four hours at the Die-Hard 500 at Talladega didn't stop Jeff Gordon from winning on the fastest track on the Winston Cup circuit. There were two major accidents during the race involving a total of twenty-five cars, one of which resulted in Dale Earnhardt's car sliding on its roof—causing Dale to suffer a broken collarbone and chestbone. When NASCAR called the race due to darkness, Gordon won in a five-lap sprint to the finish. It was his sixth win of 1996, and the win put him at the top of the point standings. Jeff was obviously a happy driver. "This is a really, really exciting win for us. To take the points lead, that's just unbelievable. . . ."

After the win at Talladega, Jeff had a total of six wins for the season and the most victories of anybody in the field in 1996. He also had the most poles with five; most laps and miles led; and most times as lap leader.

The next race on the circuit was one of Jeff's favorites but another heart-stopping crash put an end to his hope to win the third Brickyard 400. They had a few problems during the test runs at the Brickyard, but nothing that loomed as a major problem, and he qualified for the pole position in the August 3 race. He went to the front at the beginning of the race, but soon he began to feel the car was handling a little loose and the other cars were pulling close behind. Jeff decided to stay where he was until the next pit stop—when the crew could make some adjustments. Suddenly, before Jeff knew what was happening, the car was headed into the wall and Number 24 slammed hard; fortunately Jeff held control. He didn't know what caused the crash until they discovered afterward it was a cut tire that forced him into the wall. Dale Jarrett was the victor at the Brickyard, marking his third win of 1996, and his seventh NASCAR career win.

If the Brickyard was a disappointment for Jeff, it was worse for his ever-present competition, Dale Earnhardt. The injuries he suffered earlier at Talladega kept him from practicing for the Brickyard 400 at Indianapolis, although he was able to race in qualifying rounds. After beginning the Brickyard 400, however, he was forced to turn his team's driving over to Mike Skinner when physical problems overcame him. It wasn't easy, physically or emotionally, for Earnhardt to get out of the car. He said, "This is my life, right here. . . ." Still, he wisely didn't take the chance of injuring himself even more or posing a danger to others on the track.

At the twentieth race of the season, the Bud at the Glen at Watkins Glen, New York, Earnhardt qualified for the pole position and he led fifty-four laps to finish in sixth place. Geoff Bodine wound up winning at his hometown track. Jeff started in fifth and ended in fourth place at the Glen.

It was Dale Jarrett's win at the GM Goodwrench 400. Jeff came in fourth. With only ten races left on the NASCAR season circuit, Labonte led in the points standings, with Gordon and Earnhardt following in second and third, respectively.

One example of the driver/crew chief strategy that has to be worked out and why racing takes brains in addition to driving skill and mechanical ability came September

1 at the Mountain Dew Southern 500 at Darlington, South Carolina. The race came down to a duel between Jeff in Number 24 and Hut Stricklin in Number 8, with Jeff pushing hard to keep up. Ray and Jeff worked to get a greater run on each set of tires. That meant Jeff was going ten to twelve laps farther between tire changes than Stricklin, which is important because every second spent in the pit is a second not spent racing. What Ray planned was to outdistance the opposition on the final pit stop and that's what they did. Jeff won the race.

Labor Day weekend racing in Darlington found Dale Jarrett in a unique position. He became only the fourth driver ever to have a chance at the Winston Million, a prize package of $1 million to be awarded to the driver who won three of four races— the Daytona 500 (the most prestigious), the spring race at Talladega (the fastest), the Coca-Cola 600 at Charlotte (the longest), and the Southern 500 (the oldest). It had been accomplished only once previously, by Bill Elliott in 1985—earning Elliott the nickname "Million Dollar Bill." Two other drivers had attempted to win the prize, Darrell Waltrip in 1989, and the now-deceased Davey Allison in 1992. Jarrett had already won the Daytona and Charlotte races in 1996, and would have won the purse at Talladega's spring race had he not finished second to Sterling Marlin.

Alas, luck was not on Jarrett's side. In spite of a strong start in the pole position, Jarrett lost his chances for $1 million when he hit the wall on turn number three of lap number fifty-four, setting him back two full laps. And of course Jeff Gordon wound up winning, his third win in a row at Darlington and his seventh win of 1996.

A few weeks later, Jeff did it again at the MBNA 500 at Dover Downs International Speedway. His eighth win of 1996 put him back in first place in the points standings. Although feeling good about the win, he cautioned his team and his fans, "There's still plenty of races to go. Anything can happen. We're just gonna think about doing our job and doing the best job that we can. That's what we did today, and it paid off."

Gordon would win his ninth race of 1996 at the next stop on the NASCAR circuit, the Goody's Headache 500 held at Martinsville Speedway. Gordon said, "I tell you, this is a meaningful win right here. Wow . . . a complete day!" In spite of clutch problems in the same race, Terry Labonte finished in a strong second place, a tribute to his pit crew.

The North Wilkesboro Speedway held its

last NASCAR race ever with the running of the Tyson Holly Farms 400. It was a nostalgic day, to be sure, and many drivers reflected on the rich legacies. Ernie Irvan was sentimental about one particular run on the speedway: "It was unbelievable—I could hear the fans cheering me on when I was qualifying. The noise of the motor didn't drown the fans out. . . . The racetrack goes away, but we're gonna have a lot of memories [left]." In the end, Jeff Gordon would be the victor at the final Wilkesboro race and he said, "That's why I'm so excited. . . . It's been crazy this year. To be the last Winston Cup race that's gonna be here!"

Jeff raced in five meets during the month of September and won four of them. October, however, did not start well, with the UAW-GM Quality 500 at Concord, North Carolina. Jeff started at number two, but ended in the back of the pack at thirty-first because of engine problems. Terry Labonte cruised to a huge win, narrowing Gordon's lead in the points standings to just a single point. Ricky Rudd won the next race, the AC Delco 400 at Rockingham, and Bobby Hamilton won the Slick 50 500 at Phoenix. Jeff came in a disappointing twelfth at Rockingham and fifth in Phoenix.

Atlanta played host to the NAPA 500,

and Terry Labonte, Jeff Gordon, and Dale Jarrett were all in contention to win the coveted Winston Cup. However, Terry Labonte needed only to finish eighth or better to become the 1996 NASCAR champion. He subsequently finished in fifth place—clinching the Winston Cup for the first time since 1984. The win was all the more meaningful for the entire Labonte family as his brother, Bobby, won the NAPA 500. Jeff started in the number two position and finished third. Very close, but not good enough to win the Winston Cup the second year in a row.

Jeff lost the Winston Cup by only thirty-seven points to Terry Labonte but, even so, Jeff was the big money winner for the year. The final standings for 1996 were:

Name	Points	Wins	Top 5	Money Won
1. Terry Labonte	4657	2	21	$1,939,213
2. Jeff Gordon	4620	10	21	2,484,518
3. Dale Jarrett	4568	4	17	2,343,750
4. Dale Earnhardt	4327	2	13	1,725,396
5. Mark Martin	4278	0	14	1,550,555
6. Ricky Rudd	3845	1	5	1,213,313
7. Rusty Wallace	3717	5	8	1,296,912
8. Sterling Marlin	3682	2	5	1,315,050
9. Bobby Hamilton	3639	1	3	954,625
10. Ernie Irvan	3632	2	12	1,480,167

The cold statistics reveal some interesting anomalies about the way Winston Cup racing is scored. Notice, for example, that Jeff is the clear winning racer—he won ten races but came in second in the overall score to Terry Labonte, who won only two races. This is a common phenomenon in many scoring systems that reward those who consistently come in second or third as contrasted to those who either win big or lose big, which is the Jeff Gordon story for 1996. In both cases, owner Rick Hendrick is the winner since Labonte and Gordon are both his teams.

The NASCAR points system began in 1975 and was designed by Bob Latford. It is supposed to give incentives to teams for being out front in races or finishing near the front. It also strives to reward consistency. For example:

Finishes: Cars finishing in the top ten are rewarded as follows: The top five receive a five-point spread between each car and the car that follows. The next five finishers get a four-point bonus. The rest of the field gets three points between each finisher.

So the driver who finishes 1st gets	175 points	(5-point spread)
The driver who finishes 2nd gets	170 points	
3rd gets	165	
4th	160	
5th	155	

6th	150	(4-point spread)
7th	146	
8th	142	
9th	138	
10th	134	
11th	130	(3-point spread)
12th	127	
13th	124	
14th	121	
15th	118	

And so on, to the end.

Bonuses: A driver can get bonus points for leading a lap in the race. Each driver who leads at least one lap gets a five-point bonus. The driver who leads the most number of laps in a race gets another five-point bonus.

Ties: If the season ends in a tie, the number of wins is used to break the tie. If that doesn't do it, the number of second-place finishes or third-place finishes or fourth-place finishes are counted until the tie is broken.

7

1997—Jeff's NASCAR Year Six

An indication of the exploding popularity of NASCAR was the addition of two new tracks for 1997: the Texas Motor Speedway and the California Speedway. Beyond that, tracks in Las Vegas, Kansas, and Colorado were under discussion plus expansion plans overseas in Japan.

As January 1997 came around, it was time to get ready for the Daytona, but it wasn't easy for the Rainbow Warriors. Their boss, Rick Hendrick, was diagnosed with bone cancer. The big names in NASCAR showed their support for Rick Hendrick as he was fighting to save his life. NASCAR president Bill France Jr., along with car owners Roger Penske, Joe Gibbs, and Felix Sabates and drivers Terry Labonte, Jeff Gordon, Ricky Craven, Rusty Wallace, Dale Earnhardt, Ken Schrader, Bill Elliott, and Darrell Waltrip gathered at the Daytona International

Speedway and launched a program to build support for a national bone marrow transplant program. At present, Hendrick is diagnosed as having myelogenous leukemia and is undergoing treatment everyone hopes will stop the cancer. If not, a bone marrow transplant is the next alternative, and while all of his family has been tested, none has the correct matching marrow. The NASCAR idea is to build a national bone marrow computer database with millions of tested volunteers in it so marrow matching can be much easier and quicker. The number to call about the program is 1-800-MARROW2 and it will be prominently displayed on Jeff Gordon's car and the other cars in the Hendrick stable.

Ironically, in July 1991, when Ray Evernham's son, Ray Jr., was stricken with leukemia, it was Rick Hendrick who arranged and paid for treatment that put the boy on the road to recovery. That's one of the reasons the bond among the Rainbow Warriors is so close.

Still, the best way to cope was to push on with getting ready for the 1997 season. Jeff and the other Hendrick teams wanted to pay tribute to the seriously ill Rick Hendrick. The three Hendrick drivers—Jeff Gordon, Terry Labonte, and Ricky Craven—wanted to

drive to win for their team owner, who could
not attend the Daytona 500. And drive they
did, finishing a spectacular first, second, and
third. The winner was Jeff, who, (and it was
getting to be an old story by this time) at
twenty-five, was the youngest winner in the
Daytona 500's history.

Even so, it was a close win because Bill
Elliott in Number 94 was stiff competition.
There was also a multicar wreck on the final
laps with oil splattered across the track and
everybody driving under a yellow flag warn-
ing. Moments later, Jeff's teammates, Labonte and Craven, showed up in his rearview
mirror and the only driver who moved ahead
of them was Bill Elliott. Jeff felt having his
two teammates there was a good sign. He
punched on his radio and switched to teammate Terry Labonte's channel. He said,
"Terry, it would be pretty neat if we could get
these three Hendrick cars by Elliott." Terry
responded enthusiastically and Jeff clicked
over to Ricky's channel and told him their
plan. Ricky said he would be right behind
them. Jeff edged inside. Then he pushed
hard to pass Elliott on the inside and at the
same instant Terry and Ricky swung around
to pass Elliott on the outside. He couldn't
block all of those onrushing Hendrick cars
and couldn't decide fast enough which one

he would move against. In less time than it takes to tell the tale, all the Hendrick cars were in the lead as a trio.

When it was all over, crew chief Ray Evernham dialed up the boss and said, "Hey, boss, you said all we had to do was finish one-two-three in the Daytona 500. What's my next job?" The delighted but ailing Hendrick popped back, "You're gonna have to run the car dealerships."

The fourth race of the season brought the Jeff Gordon team something it didn't want, its first DNF (Did Not Finish). Jeff said the car seemed fine at the outset of the race and he was moving up through the pack when he felt it explode. The engine had blown and that was the end of the racing day.

Jeff placed a dismal thirtieth in the debut race at the Texas Motor Speedway. The next week he came back big with a win in the Food City 500. The race was difficult—there were twenty caution flags, a track record. He did it again on April 20 at the Goody's Headache Powder 500 at Martinsville. Going into May, Jeff had won four big Cup races.

Beyond all the excitement of the actual race, the typical race day is an interesting marshaling of men and machines. The garage area is opened up at seven in the morning when the traveling crew sets up equipment and cars so the pit crew can start work. (There are two kinds of crews on race day: the traveling crew and the pit crew.) The traveling crew is at the track for several days before the actual race while the car and driver go through the practice sessions to get a feel for the track and for the car on that particular track. Also, they are there for the pole-qualifying laps. The pit crew, the Rainbow Warriors in Jeff's case, arrive at the track the day of the race at eight A.M. Some of them go to the garage stall, where Number 24 has been overnight, and begin to unpack it—to peel back the tarps and other wrappings that have been protecting the car.

The night before, Ray Evernham (and all the other racing crew chiefs) worked out the crew setup for race day, made up a checklist of everything that has to be done, and assigned each task to some member of the crew.

For example, the shocks are set to suit racing mode with springs inserted; spoiler and car heights are adjusted; all the oils are changed; and all the equipment such as driver's controls and the radio are checked for proper working condition. Then the car is polished. This is not for appearance but, rather, to make the car as smooth as possible so as to reduce air friction during the race. For the same reason, tape is stripped over certain places on the grille to cut air resistance.

After all this is done, the inspectors come around and make a final check of the car to make sure it complies with NASCAR regulations. When the inspectors are done and satisfied, they put a sticker on the car and no further major changes are allowed to be made by the crew. At that point, a heater is connected to the lubrication system to heat up the oil in the engine and make it as slick as possible from the very start. Then the car is moved out onto the line.

Who gets what pit is determined by how the various teams' cars qualified, with the fastest qualifier getting the choice of his pit, the second-fastest qualifier getting second choice, and so on. The crew then goes over to its pit and gets set up. Each crew sets up its pit the same way for every race so everybody knows just where every tool is, where the tires are, the gasoline, and so on. The all-important tires are arranged in matched sets; the pressure checked then and throughout the race. The pit crew members whose specialty is to change tires run out their air hose lines and check their air guns; the special NASCAR gas cans are filled; the computers and other equipment are set up and tested.

The month of May was good to Jeff Gordon. May 4 at the Sears Point Raceway in Sonoma, California, saw him finishing second. A week later in Talladega, he drove to a fifth-place finish.

At the time of the Coca-Cola 600 in late May, Ray Evernham spoke out about a change in NASCAR rules that he thought gave the Ford teams an unfair edge against Jeff's Chevy Monte Carlo. This is an illustration of how much NASCAR rules can affect a race. NASCAR decided to add a quarter inch to the rear spoilers on the Ford Thunderbirds at the Coca-Cola 600 coming up at the Charlotte track. This meant the Fords would have more down force at the rear of the car, giving it better rear-wheel traction, and a racing advantage. Evernham protested that dynamometer and wind-tunnel tests showed the Fords already had more horsepower and more down force. The crew chief saw this as an admission by Ford teams and drivers that they can't beat Jeff Gordon in a fair race.

"This is not about making the cars equal. This is like putting twenty-pound ankle weights on Michael Jordan. . . . Ford is admitting that on an equal basis they can't beat Hendrick Motorsports."

When all was said and done, Jeff performed beautifully. He started the race at the number one pole position and crossed to the checkered flag.

Jeff was fighting to keep the lead in the Winston Cup competition. By the time he got to the Jiffy Lube 300 in Loudon, New Hampshire, for the July 13 race he had chalked up two more first-place finishes, as well as a fifth, since the Coca-Cola 600. He had won seven times so far, but had a lead of only fifty-four points ahead of teammate Terry Labonte. His race in New Hampshire was hurt by a poor qualifying run that pushed him to the twenty-ninth starting position. Jeff crossed the finish line twenty-third.

Toward the end of July at the Pocono track in Long Pond, Pennsylvania, Jeff came up against a surprisingly strong Dale Jarrett at the Pennsylvania 500 as the two battled back and forth to claim the lead spot. They traded the number one position four times, and finally, Jarrett pulled away in lap 180 and won by 2.99 seconds. It was Jarrett's third win of the season and the eleventh win for a Ford car out of eighteen tries in the season so far. On the plus side for Jeff, he had seven wins so far in his Monte Carlo and regained

Tom Copeland

THE ROAD TO VICTORY IN ATLANTA

The Rainbow Warriors servicing Jeff's car during the final 1997
Winston Cup race

Tom Copeland (2)

The Warriors cheer as Jeff crosses the finish line

David Taylor/ALLSPORT (2)

One of the highlights of Jeff's career was winning the first
Brickyard 400 in 1994 at the famed Indianapolis Speedway

Tom Copeland

Jeff and Brooke (left) flash winning smiles in the winner's circle at the Goodwrench 400

Start of Goody's Headache Powder 500, which ended with another checkered flag for DuPont Number 24

Jeff passes Rusty Wallace for the win at the Coca-Cola 600

Tom Copeland (3)

INSIDE
THE GORDON GARAGE

Jeff chats with a crew member . . .

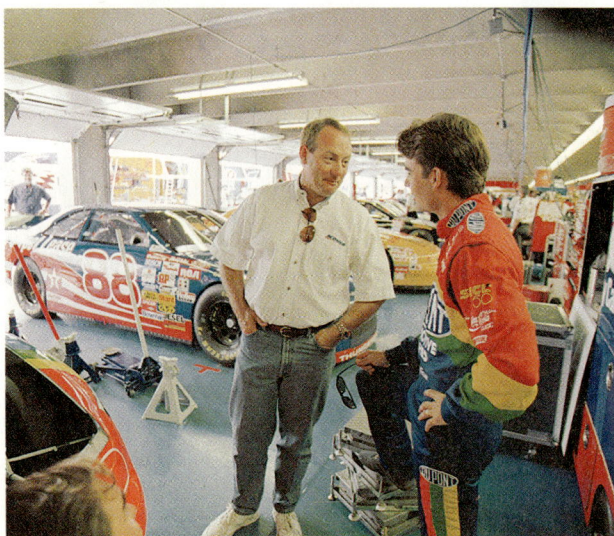

Tom Copeland (2)

. . . and with fellow driver Ken Schrader

Tom Copeland

Crew chief Ray Evernham celebrates
the team's second Winston Cup championship

David Taylor/ALLSPORT

his lead in the race for the Winston Cup after having lost it earlier to Hendrick Motorsports teammate Terry Labonte, last year's winner.

At the Pocono race, the importance of the pit crew's ability and the crew chief's judgment was demonstrated again for Jeff as he realized he was coming down with a flat tire and radioed Evernham. Ray called for all four tires to be changed at the next pit stop and that was done so fast that Jeff was able to get back out on the track and stay in front of the leader. Later in that race, Jeff felt that a front tire was going down and called in to Ray. Jeff's inclination was to make a pit stop and change tires again, but Ray said the tires looked fine and to keep going. From what Jeff was reporting about the handling of the car, Ray believed Jeff had run over some chunks of rubber on the track. Jeff could have picked some up and spun them out again. So Ray told him to select a different groove on the track in which to run and that turned the trick.

The next three races of the season were solid ones for Jeff Gordon: a fourth-place finish at the Brickyard 400, the checkered flag at the Bud on the Glen in New York, and second place at the ITW Devilbiss 400. On

August 23, Jeff probably had a huge headache in Bristol, Tennessee. At the Goody's Headache Powder he crossed the finish line in thirty-fifth place.

A big turnaround was in store for Jeff with the race for the Winston Million on August 31 at the Darlington Raceway. To win the Winston Million, a driver has to get the checkered flag on three out of four designated races in the year—the Daytona, Charlotte, Talladega, and Darlington. Jeff was on the verge of doing just that, having won the Daytona 500 and the Coca Cola 600. All he had to do was win the Mountain Dew Southern 500 at Darlington and he'd make his mark in history and put a million dollars in the bank.

The Mountain Dew Southern 500 made history for Jeff Gordon and racing in several ways, climaxing with one of the most exciting race endings in a long time. Jeff won himself a million dollars by the skin-of-the-teeth margin of .144 seconds, barely edging out Jeff Burton. The duel between the two Jeffs went to the last lap. As the drivers moved into the turn, Burton slipped around Gordon's inside with the two bumping metal. Gordon held to the outside and charged ahead just enough to earn the checkered flag and the million dollars. Gordon said he knew the ending was going to be close and he had to summon up every bit of his "refuse-to-lose" spirit.

Burton later said that Jeff had cut down on him and he could have cut back and wrecked him, but he didn't want to win that way. He said if he had been going for the million bucks, he might have done the same thing. "Gordon was racing for a million dollars. You can't blame the guy," said Burton.

It was a dramatic finish and a narrow win for a dramatic reward. It also put Jeff Gordon back on top in the race for the 1997 Winston Cup National Championship.

One of the alarming things that happened during the Southern 500 as Jeff was dashing to the million-dollar prize was an unexpected blackout by Dale Earnhardt. Doctors who examined him later said that it may have been caused by his unusually low heart rate, which tends to drop even more under stress. The neurosurgeon who examined him said the blackout was due to a cardiovascular problem that is consistent with Earnhardt's family's history. Dale said he was determined to be in the Exide Batteries Select 400 on the Richmond track September 9. Jeff was there, too, starting tenth and finishing third, behind Dale Jarrett and Jeff

Burton. Dale Earnhardt placed sixth and said that he felt fine during the race.

Then it was on to the CMT 300, where Jeff racked up another win after starting in the thirteenth position. This was his *tenth* win of the season, which surprised even him. "It's amazing that we have won ten races this season," he said. "The competition has been real tough." With that win, Jeff became the first driver in fifteen years of NASCAR racing to have a season with a double-digit victory record.

The next race was the MBNA 400 at Dover, Delaware, where Mark Martin demonstrated how tough Jeff's competition was: he won the pole position by just .0039 seconds. Martin eventually won the race; Jeff finished seventh.

At the Hanes 500 at Martinsville, Virginia, the winner was the other Jeff—Jeff Burton. Rusty Wallace was penalized for going too fast, shooting past the pace car before it had left the track; Wallace had to return to the pit. Burton pulled ahead and held off a challenge by Dale Earnhardt, who finished second, followed by Bobby Hamilton, and Jeff Gordon coming in fourth.

The 1997 season neared the end; there were five races left. Jeff Gordon was ahead of Mark Martin by 135 points in the race for the Winston Cup trophy. The UAW-GM 500 at Concord, North Carolina, saw Jeff qualifying at the fourth pole position, but there were some other developments. Everybody was stunned when Darrell Waltrip didn't qualify and didn't make the cut. He was so depressed that he and his Number 17 crew left the speedway without talking to anyone. Also surprising was Geoff Bodine's pulling down the pole position, because his driving had been mixed all year.

At that point Jeff needed to finish fourth or better in the five remaining races of the season to cinch the Winston Cup for a second time. He ran fifth at the UAW-GM Quality 500.

October 12 brought the kind of race in the Sears Die-Hard 500 at Talladega, Alabama, in front of 130,000 spectators that no one likes. Jeff got messed up in a crazy 21-car smashup when his left rear tire went to shreds on lap 140, running at about 190 miles per hour. "I felt the left rear go just before my car turned sideways. Then I bounced off car ninety-eight and just went spinning." Luckily, no one was hurt and the race ended with Terry Labonte the winner and Gordon coming in thirty-fifth.

The AC-Delco 400 was an unusual race because it was close and a hard-fought finish. The race was postponed a day at the Rock—North Carolina Motor Speedway in Rockingham, North Carolina—because of rain, but on Monday, October 27, everybody was off and running. The lead changed twenty times until lap 378 when Bobby Hamilton took the lead for the last time. On the very last lap, Dale Jarrett slipped into second place, followed by Ricky Craven. Jeff Gordon crossed the finish line in the fourth position.

Two more races to go and the 1997 Winston Cup Series championship was still undecided. The point spread among the leaders was so close that every lap, every pole position, and every pit stop became important enough to make the difference. On November 2, at the Dura-Lube 500, on the Avondale track near Phoenix, Arizona, Jeff qualified for only the number twelve starting position. Something that highlights the razor-thin precision of motor racing is the fact that Bobby Hamilton, who garnered the pole position at the Dura-Lube 500, did it at a speed of 131.579 miles per hour; Jeff was relegated to the number twelve spot going 129.898 miles per hour—1.681 miles per hour slower!

On the day of the race, Jeff had mechanical trouble again, and Dale Jarrett got the checkered flag, which moved him up in the Winston Cup points standings to just 77 points behind Jeff. Mark Martin was edged out of second place and dropped to third position, trailing Jeff by 87. Jarrett was one happy driver: with one more race to go, the odds had shortened. As he said, "Well, we've got a chance, and that's all we asked for . . . to have a shot at it."

Of course, Jeff was one unhappy driver. He was driving a strong race in the 312-lap Dura-Lube when he began having trouble with a wheel after 200 laps. He recovered momentarily and rocketed by Rusty Wallace into the lead and stayed in the top five until the 273rd lap. Then he had another problem. It happened as Jarrett lapped him, and Jeff's right front tire cut, throwing the car into a slide and almost slamming it into the wall on the third turn. "I really don't know what the problem was. I felt something was going on the right side, and I knew it was going to be a miracle to get to the end without pitting. Then, bang, something just went. I was real lucky not to hit the wall." Jeff was able to regain control quickly but was forced into the pit for repair. When he slipped back onto the track, it was in the thirtieth position. Years of driving know-how came into play, and he was able to weave and slip through the pack to finish seventeenth.

Jeff was still in the lead for overall points, but the margin between him and the others in the top five slots had narrowed significantly. He had to finish eighteenth or higher in Atlanta two weeks later in order to clinch the cup, but in a sport as unpredictable and volatile as NASCAR racing, that was not a sure thing. Particularly since Jeff was plagued not with driving mistakes but with mechanical failures. "We've had two flat tires in the last three races, and that's pretty unfortunate. I've said all year this championship is going to come down to Atlanta. That's pretty much what we've got right now."

It may have been a little psychological warfare, but what both Jarrett and Martin told reporters four days before the Atlanta race was true, namely that the Winston Cup championship was Jeff's to lose, not theirs to win. Jarrett said, "No matter what happens this weekend, we'll look back on 1997 and say we had a great time, we accomplished a lot of things that we set out to accomplish." Martin chimed in to say that "If they [the DuPont team] don't have a problem, they won't lose that championship because they won't run bad enough to lose it."

Martin put his finger on the crux of this final and championship-deciding race, because when he refers to a "problem," he is talking about mechanical failure, not Jeff's driving ability. It was mechanical failure that bedeviled the DuPont team. And while Jeff won ten races, he also finished farther behind eighteenth in seven races, so it was not as cut and dried as Jarrett and Martin might want everybody to think. Other factors to consider were that the Atlanta track in 1997 was a different track from the one everybody had raced on in previous years because it had been repaved and reconfigured to make it much faster. The test laps run on the track after these changes produced speeds of over 190 mph. There was also a serious possibility of rain on the day of the race. There were new factors that had to be figured into this final and decisive race.

When the time came for the qualifying races, Dale Jarrett racked up the third starting position with a 195.115 mph lap; Mark Martin was set to start ninth with his 194.077 mph lap. What Jeff racked up was trouble. It was a very cold morning as he started down the pit road at 8:30, and he wiggled his tires to warm them up and scuff them for better traction. He was starting out onto the main track when, all of a sudden, his car got away from him for a moment; he slid sideways and rammed Bobby Hamilton, who was also on the pit road. The result was that both Hamilton and Jeff had to return to their pits and switch to backup cars. This delay also cut into the time for practice laps. Following this, Jeff got onto the track to do his qualifying lap, and the car got away from him again. It began slipping and sliding on some loose junk or oil on the track surface, and Jeff never did quite get things under control. He had a poor qualifying run. His car was running looser than it should have been, wobbling into the turns and forcing Jeff to ease up on the gas pedal, which cut his speed and qualifying time. At the end of the qualifying runs, Jeff's speed was 190.673, which put him in thirty-seventh position in an array of forty-three cars. That was his worst starting position of the entire season, and in contrast, Jarrett pulled down the third spot and Martin the ninth.

The irony is that the loose junk on the track during the qualifying run might have come from Jeff's own car. "There was something on the racetrack, and I think it might have come from our car. That's what happens when you get rushed like this." Jeff says that Ray Evernham always tells him when things like this happen that it could have been worse. That's true, but it doesn't mean Jeff likes it.

Then came the dawning of Sunday, November 16, 1997. Ray Evernham looked Jeff in the eye and told him, "Our chance to win this race went away yesterday. So what we have to do is win the championship." That meant finishing in the top eighteen. When it was over, Bobby Labonte was the race winner, Dale Jarrett and Mark Martin had made laudable runs finishing second and third, while an elated Jeff finished seventeenth and won the championship for the second time in three years. It was a great boost for the ailing team owner, Rick Hendrick, because it was his third team championship in a row.

Starting way back in the pack at thirty-seventh, Jeff threaded his way forward, forward, ever forward, slipping past competitors and pushing as hard as he dared. He had to be very careful because of all the bad luck that had dogged him and the Rainbow Warriors in recent days, and he didn't want to lose the race through some thoughtless error. As the race roared on and on through its three hundred laps, Jeff and Ray maintained contact on the radio, plotting their tactics and exchanging thoughts. They both agreed that they had not been able to synch the car's setup quite right for this day and this track. It was giving Jeff handling problems, and they both worried about the tires. Ray kept cautioning him to save the right rear tire by driving carefully. Jeff was worried because his car was driving too loosely, and he was afraid that if anyone got close enough to force him to brake or shift suddenly the car would spin out and end the race for the Winston Cup. Finally, Ray agreed Jeff should come in with fifty-six laps to go. They put on another set of tires, which barely made it through to the end of the race.

It was a grueling race for Jeff and Ray Evernham because they were both so intensely focused on every detail and every whisper of trouble that might sink their dream. Jeff said it was one of the most stressful days of his life. "When I crossed the finish line, it was the biggest sigh of relief," Jeff said afterward. Ray agreed. "It was one of the most stressful weekends I've ever had, but everybody did what they had to do today."

When it finally ended, it was a win almost by a whisper, with Jeff edging Jarrett out by only 14 points out of a total of 4,610! They brought out the champagne, and a thankful Brooke was next to Jeff in Victory Lane. As he raised his second NASCAR Winston Cup Series championship trophy over his head, 152,000 cheering fans punctuated his extraordinary victory.

Martin was only fifteen points shy of Jarrett, with the result that all three will go down in the record books as the closest one-two-three point standing finish in the history of NASCAR and the fourth-closest finish. The closest finish was in 1989, when Rusty Wallace slipped by Dale Earnhardt with a twelve-point edge; next was Richard Petty's eleven-point margin over Darrell Waltrip in 1991; and, finally, the late Alan Kulwicki beat Bill Elliot in 1992 by only ten points.

The significance of Jeff's victory can easily be lost in looking at the frustrations and aggravations of this final racing weekend—equipment failure, driver error, and misfortune. But remember, Jeff started from the worst qualifying position of his career—thirty-seventh—and was still able, with the help of the Rainbow Warriors, to maneuver his way to the championship. And the seventeenth-position finish in the final race was enough to win the cup, which attests to Jeff's long-term consistency as a skilled NASCAR driver, winning ten of the thirty-two races in the season and finishing in the top five drivers in twenty-two of those races. The championship goes to the best overall, year-long driver in thirty-two races, and that's what Jeff was.

One important indication of the kind of competitor Jeff is was revealed when he said after it was all over, "I've got to give a lot of credit to Mark Martin and Dale Jarrett because they're just the greatest competitors. They worked hard, and they deserved to win this championship every bit as much as we did. Me and Dale and Mark got together last night, held hands, and prayed. And praying and having faith had a lot to do with what we were able to do today."

Three days after winning the Winston Cup championship, Jeff went into the hospital to have a polyp successfully removed from his vocal cords. Later he went home to recover and, always the positive thinker, said, "I don't know if I planned this surgery or if God planned it for me, but I'm going to have about seven to ten days here where I'm going to be able to do a lot of thinking. I'm really looking forward to that." Doctors report this condition occurs in people who do a lot of speaking, as Jeff does in his many interviews and meetings with fans.

Three weeks after Atlanta, Jeff headed to the NASCAR Winston Cup Series Awards Banquet in New York on December 5, where there was almost $2 million in prize money waiting for him. Not a bad year at all.

8

Jeff Gordon and the Rainbow Warriors

No one has a higher regard for his crew than does Jeff Gordon for the Rainbow Warriors. Talented as Jeff Gordon is, he knows every checkered flag he gets is the result of team effort and he cannot do it alone.

It all started when owner Rick Hendrick told Ray Evernham, the chief of the Number 24 crew, to start the DuPont team in 1992. Evernham designed the ten-thousand-square-foot race shop in the Hendrick Motorsports nine-building compound near Charlotte, the largest in stock car racing. He hired the DuPont shop crew and assembled the Rainbow Warriors. The Warriors work together, regularly rehearsing what has to be done during a race, when there isn't time for mistakes. They work out together twice a week, plus run eight or ten practice pit stops at their shop every week. It's not unusual for the fifteen mechanics in the shop to work fourteen hours a day, seven days a week during the season. Among the crew is team engineer Brian Whitesell, chief mechanic Ed Guzzo, chief fabricator Pete Bingle, engine manager Jim Wall, and team aerodynamicist Gary Eaker.

Most everybody watching a NASCAR race tends to focus on what's going on out on the track, but the race may be won or lost off the track in the pit. When you analyze the outcomes of most NASCAR races, the margin of victory is often a few seconds or less. So the speed with which a pit crew can service a car when it comes in can make the difference. Jeff Gordon is fortunate in that the Rainbow Warriors can usually change four tires, clean the windshield, and fill the gas tank in less than twenty seconds.

Pit row at the side of the racetrack has, as its name indicates, a row of pits where each driver and car can get serviced by his racing team. The trouble is that there are so many pits and drivers are moving so fast, that they are not always sure where their pit is. So each team puts up a symbol or a sign to identify itself to its driver. Early in his career Jeff missed a pit stop because he couldn't locate his pit in time to slow down and pull in. Anytime a driver has to slow down and do another lap to find his pit, he can lose enough time to affect the outcome of the race. At first the Rainbow Warriors adopted a bright yellow tomahawk sign, because its first race as a team was at Atlanta, home of Ted Turner's Atlanta Braves. But as more and more crews put up signs and symbols it got harder and harder for Jeff to see even the tomahawk, so they added a rainbow banner to the tomahawk. That's what they still use today.

NASCAR rules, incidentally, don't just apply to the driver on the track; they also apply to the driver and the crew on the pit stops, regulating who can do what, where, and when. Here are some of the rules and the penalties for breaking them. NASCAR is not forgiving and no warnings are given. If you break the rule, intentionally or accidentally, you are penalized.

If your car is over the front line of the pit box	1 lap penalty
If your car is out of the pit box on the right side	1 lap penalty
If you pass or race on the pit road	Go to end of longest line
If you pit out of order	Go to end of longest line
If you have more than 7 men over the wall	15-second penalty per man
If your crew is over the wall too soon	15 seconds
If you run over an air hose	Go back in the pit

If you run over a jack	Go back in the pit

To get some idea of the impact of orchestrated pit stops, you have only to review NASCAR's own records on the average time it took to change four tires and refill the twenty-two-gallon gas tank over the years.

In 1950, the average pit stop took   4 minutes
In 1960, this was cut way down to   49 seconds
In 1970, it was reduced to   35 seconds
In 1980, this was trimmed to   30 seconds
In 1990, it was shaved to   22 seconds
In 1997, it was down to   20 seconds

A pit stop works like this: before the car pulls in, the pit crew are over the wall and in position in two lines so the car can pull in between them. As the car pulls in, one crewman holds up a marker to show the driver exactly where to stop. The jack man is at the right side and jacks up the car in one or two pumps of the lever; the tire changers undo the wheel lugs, pull off the tire, and mount the new tire. As this is going on, the two gas men are pouring eleven gallons of gas into the tank and watching for dangerous gasoline spills. At the same time, one crewman is cleaning the grille with a brush on a long pole. All of this should not take more than ten seconds. Then the jack man drops the car and, picking up the jack, races around to the driver's side of the car, where he and the tire-changing crew repeat what they just did on the right side. Meanwhile, the gas men pour in another eleven gallons of gasoline or whatever is needed to fill the tank. Another crewman cleans the windshield and gives the driver water to drink if he needs it. Within twenty seconds or less, everybody is finished, the jack man lowers the driver's side of the car, and the driver pulls out onto the track again. This is a maneuver he must do properly because if a driver leaves or reenters the track too fast or too slowly after a pit stop he could be penalized by NASCAR officials.

The seventy-five-pound tires cost about $1,200 each and are supplied the day before the race by Goodyear. A team can use as many as they want, but the average is from $18,000 to $20,000 worth of tires per race. Alongside the pit is the "war wagon," which has all the tools the crew may need. In addition, the crew has a small computer set to receive signals from race officials about the speed and position of each car in the race based on information from a transponder mounted on the car. Other electronic equipment includes a TV camera that tapes every pit stop so the crew can later review what and how it did. The crew chief and driver are also in touch on two-way radio to help plan the race, but this is a mixed blessing since anybody can tune in to the team's frequency. This is simple enough for the fans to do and many of them are listening on their radios as the race progresses, but opposing teams can also tune in and learn what a team is doing.

Beyond that, there is complex interaction between driver and crew chief. During the several hours of grueling tension drivers spend on the track maneuvering, there is one operation nobody can see—the crew chief and driver are constantly analyzing the situation on the track and making judgments about strategy. The two are constantly talking on the radio, deciding when to make a pit stop and whether to change tires and fill up on fuel. That decision affects other drivers. Those cars on top of you will probably also make pit stops because they won't lose much time or position relative to you. Those farther behind may try to stay in the race because they have more time and distance to make up. Other considerations include what's happening on the track at the moment. For example, when there is a caution flag, drivers will often zoom into the pit because they can usually go in and out without seriously affecting their position in the race.

Aside from all the help Jeff gets from the Rainbow Warriors, he still has to depend on himself. For openers, Jeff has to know just how to start his Number 24 DuPont Monte Carlo—and it isn't as simple as turning the key in the family car. Instead, there are a number of switches and buttons within reach. Two of them are safety switches that Jeff always hopes he will never have to use. Both would be used in a serious crash. One is the master override switch that kills all the electricity in the car instantly so as to avoid a spark that could trigger a gasoline fire. The other is the fire safety switch that immediately activates a fire-extinguisher to spray all over Jeff. A button he does press a lot is the radio button he uses to communicate with Ray Evernham during the race.

But when it comes to race time, Jeff not only has to know what to do in the complicated starting procedure, but when to do it. If he jumps the gun, so to speak, he can be penalized. So before hearing the command, "Start your engines!" Jeff trips several toggle switches to put Number 24 into the ready position. These include the battery, tachometer, and voltmeter switches, in that order. Then comes the switch to get the engine turning over and, at the instant the command comes from the official, the start switch. At that point he has some seven hundred plus horsepower at his command and he is ready to shift gears and slip into first to start moving behind the pace car. He has to control the transmission and shift smoothly because his car can get up to sixty-five miles per hour in low gear if he lets it, which, of course, he doesn't.

It is a fast ride and it has the unique aspect of constantly making left turns because all American races are run counterclockwise—nothing but left turns. The car is set up by the team to turn left by the way the tires are installed; the driver has to be careful that the car doesn't keep turning left and ram into the infield. He must constantly adjust and correct the steering. The car also has a stiff suspension to take the strain of racing and this makes bumps rougher. To help ease the 140-plus-degree temperatures that form inside the car, Gordon can activate an air-blower system that circulates outside air into his helmet and also blows away some of the carbon monoxide gas that might collect in the cab of the car.

Sometimes a driver will play his wheels back and forth a little to warm the tires, then with his five-point seat harness on as tight as possible, he will start rolling down the track. When the pace car releases control of the track and the green flag signaling the start of the race goes down, so does Jeff's foot on the gas pedal, and the tachometer races to eight thousand or more revolutions per minute as Jeff shifts gears and zooms down the track amid other cars doing the same thing.

Tires are a driving and car-handling factor that is critical. Tires that are too worn can significantly pull down the speed of a car. All the tires used at NASCAR events are supplied by Goodyear to NASCAR specifications. The crew chiefs know that they can affect the handling of the car and, perhaps, the outcome of the race by altering the pressure in each tire. This often relates to the kind of track being run. For example, here is the kind of tire pressure that might typically be used on different tracks:

	Superspeedway	Intermediate	Short
Left Front	45 lbs.	30 lbs.	18 lbs.
Right Front	55	48	28
Left Rear	45	30	18
Right Rear	50	43	28

Notice that the tire pressures on each side of the car tend to be nearly equal. On the short track, where there are many turns, the pressure tends to be significantly lower than on the superspeedway and intermediate tracks. At times, crew chiefs will also mount different-size tires on various wheels to get the most traction for the car. For example, since in most tracks the car is turning only to the left, mounting slightly larger tires on the right side of the car will push the car to the left easier and give it a little more speed on the turns.

Another consideration for Jeff and his team is the kind of track they are racing on at any given time. NASCAR races on four different kinds of tracks and each is different in significant ways. The driver, the car, and the crew must adjust for each. The four kinds of tracks are the superspeedway, the intermediate, the short, and the road track.

Traditionally, races in the United States run counterclockwise while races in Europe run clockwise. We don't know why this is true, only that it is and that's the way it is in NASCAR races on the first three kinds of tracks—superspeedway, intermediate, and short. In those races, therefore, the cars are always turning to the left and that's the way they are rigged. In the fourth type of race, the cars have to turn either way, which makes it a lot trickier for a driver like Jeff

Gordon, who has spent years turning left only. The road-course tracks include Sears Point in California and Watkins Glen in New York.

Superspeedways such as Daytona and Talladega are two miles or longer. Intermediate tracks, such as Dover or Atlanta, run from one to two miles in length. The short race courses are only half a mile or, perhaps, three-quarters of a mile long and they are a whole different world in racing. For one thing, obviously the laps are faster—as short as fifteen seconds on some tracks—and there is more turning, which has a big impact on the tires. Because everything is quicker, drivers commonly tap slower cars on the rear bumper to get them to move over. This is not permitted on some of the longer tracks, but it is considered commonplace on the short ones.

The racing team is made up of a number of specialists, and much of the work is done by the team at its own shop. Some work, however, is purchased from outside suppliers. There are specialists who work on the engine, the chassis, and the body. While some car racing sports use the most advanced technology, this is not true of NASCAR racing. The philosophy of NASCAR is that these are all stock cars that are in general production by car manufacturers. Theoretically, ordinary people are driving around on public streets with similar cars. That is, of course, to a certain extent fiction because they are stock cars that have been refined, honed, and tuned at the racing team's shop. The finished product is something you would never find on public streets. These are the newest refinements of the old car technology.

The fuel system illustrates this point. NASCAR racers don't use the latest fuel-injection systems but, rather, refined four-barrel carburetors using the same kind of parts that the manufacturer uses. There is no major alteration allowed except in the case of superspeedway tracks that require everybody to have restrictor plates that reduce the power of the cars. Also, NASCAR does permit certain modifications to the stock car for reasons of safety or competition. For example, Winston Cup circuit racers have a different way of handling engine oil. In the stock car from the manufacturer, the oil is pumped up from a catch pan under the engine and allowed to drain down back into that pan to be recycled again. NASCAR racers in contrast have a pump pushing the oil through the engine and car system all the time under pressure.

The suspension of the body on the chassis is very important in how the car handles. The springs that give that suspension have to be adjusted with wedges or other devices to make it best for the driver. For example, driving straight will normally have the weight of the car spread out equally on all four tires, but as the car turns left or right the weight shifts. In order for the driver to keep control of the car this shift in weight and power has to be offset by the suspension springs, and the better they do it, the more responsive and controllable the car is.

The entire team travels all season long. Some crew members do remain back at the shop working on cars for future races and some travel to the track to work on the cars and man the pit. Being on the road isn't like your basic vacation. Every team involved in the Winston Cup competition has to show up for most or all of the races and these are now spread out over more than thirty tracks in thirteen states. It's expanding all the time with Texas, California, and Las Vegas recently added to the itinerary.

Typically, a team will travel with at least two cars, plus tires, tools, spares (including spare engines), their own generators and lighting system, and a catalog of parts. To move the equipment involved, Hendrick Motorsports uses a big custom-built trailer rig that's a machine shop, kitchen, and lounge all in one. It will travel forty thousand miles per year to races and test sessions. Hendrick Motorsports has its own planes to fly approximately fifty people to the site of the next race. All in all, the business of competing in the Winston Cup costs from $3 to $5 million a year.

A lot rides on the skill and experience of Jeff and crew chief Ray Evernham and their pit boss—a six-foot four-inch ex–football player named Andy Papathanassiou. (Ray Evernham calls him a "good Irish boy.") Andy was specially trained in organizing team efforts and has a master's degree from Stanford.

Just as John Bickford was the guiding hand during Jeff Gordon's earliest years, Ray Evernham has been the hand on the tiller in recent times as Jeff challenged the world of NASCAR racing. Ray Evernham is the experienced, level head guiding Gordon down the path of NASCAR success. Evernham knows what he has in Gordon. "Nobody had to teach Michael Jordan how to play basketball, and nobody taught Jeff Gordon how to drive." Evernham said that after athletes such as Jordon and Gordon learned the fundamentals of their sport, they understood what to do with that training and used it easily and effectively. You can't do that, Evernham believes, unless you are a natural at your sport—and Gordon is a natural-born winner at race car driving.

9

Corn Whiskey and Cars:
The History and Culture
of NASCAR

The world of NASCAR existed long before Jeff Gordon was born and he did not become its current star in a vacuum. He is part of a long tradition and culture that was born half a century ago in the form of a deadly race between wild moonshiners and determined sheriffs roaring down twisting, dirt back roads. This evolved into a sport of daredevils racing in fast stock cars, which then blossomed into the National Association for Stock Car Auto Racing or NASCAR. Today, it is one of the three most popular sports in America, with five million yelling fans taking in every turn, every pit stop, every detail and nuance of NASCAR's Winston Cup races.

In many ways NASCAR and the Winston Cup Series is unique, in the true definition of that word, in the world of professional sports. The swirling masses of people, the multicolored cars and participants in their uniforms, the sense of danger and imminence of death and destruction, the sound of the engines, the speed of moving machines, the crowd noises, the smells—all contribute to a cacophony of sensory experiences unlike that found in other sports. In most other sports, we are only spectators knowing that what is happening on the field or the court is not within our personal experience. Few of us have played football, boxed a few rounds, or performed on the uneven parallel bars. In contrast, most of us drive cars that, in theory, are just like those out there on the track. Also, during the sporting event, motor racing fans are often closer to the participants than in other professional sports, and afterward, they are on the infield mingling with the teams. That happens in no other sport. During the races, for example, there is two-way radio communication between Jeff in the car and crew chief Ray Evernham in the pit, and many of the fans are listening in on this communication. In fact, the team's scanner frequencies (467.0625 and 469.4875) are given out to the fans. This would be comparable to football fans listening in on the conversations between the coach on the sideline and the quarterback on the field or the team spotter up in the press box.

Winston Cup racing's astonishing popularity comes from tangible marks of competition such as number of laps won, races won, poles won, engine statistics, gear ratios, time spent per pit stop, and so on. Beyond that is the intangible symbol connected with NASCAR racing: the romance of one man fighting to win on his own—which is the theme of heroes throughout the ages that has a particular resonance for Americans. That's the knight or the cowboy or these independent farmers distilling moonshine whiskey in secret and outracing the sheriff in their cars to get it to market. In fact, some of the early NASCAR racing stars were literally moonshiners such as Junior Johnson, Tim Flock, and Curtis Turner.

The romance of outracing revenuers is part of American popular culture in our television, movies, rock and country music, magazines, books, and trends. We have seen it, for example, in the 1990 movie *Days of Thunder*, starring Tom Cruise, Randy Quaid, and Robert Duvall. This is the story of a sprint car driver out of California who connects with a car dealer in Charlotte, and becomes a member of his racing team with the help of an experienced NASCAR veteran crew chief. The plot, written in 1989, could be a page out of the life of Jeff Gordon, detailing his becoming part of the Rick Hendrick racing empire with crew chief Ray Evernham. In real life, it *is* the story of Rick Hendrick and one of his earlier teams. Three years after the movie came out, it happened all over again when Jeff Gordon and Ray Evernham joined the Hendrick organization.

Many professionals in NASCAR, incidentally, hated *Days of Thunder* because it pandered to the outdated stereotype of NASCAR men as moonshine-swilling, skirt-chasing, racist bums. In fact, today they are very high-tech professionals with advanced college degrees who live notoriously circumspect lives, which is why Jeff Gordon has become the poster boy of NASCAR for the twenty-first century.

It's interesting to see how NASCAR was born out of the dream of one man. The key name in NASCAR racing is France—the man, not the country. William Henry Getty France was intrigued by racing as he grew up in the sleepy little southern town that was Washington, D.C. France, who was born in Washington in 1909, was drawn to cars and started tinkering with them as a boy and grew up to be a car mechanic. One of the more entertaining things a young man could do in those days was to go to the dirt racetracks in nearby Virginia and Maryland.

During these years, Bill fell in love with three things. The first was cars and car racing; the second was Anne Bledsoe whom he met at a dance and soon married; the third was Daytona Beach, Florida.

In the early years of his marriage, Bill continued as a car mechanic and a racing fan, to the point that he even had a car to race at the nearby tracks. Soon the Frances had a son, William, and decided to move south. So they piled everything into the car and headed down the road toward Florida. When they got to Daytona Beach, Bill and Anne liked the place immediately and decided that was as far south as they wanted to go. One of the attractions when they arrived in 1934 was the Sir Malcolm Campbell speed show that drew a lot of tourist money for the town. It was a blow when Campbell moved on to the Utah salt flats two years later.

At first, the Daytona city fathers tried to substitute a car race to continue attracting the tourists and France entered the race that was run partly on the highway and partly on the sand of the beach. He finished fifth. Unfortunately, the idea was a money-loser because the racetrack was poorly laid out and it wasn't a very good race. When the city officials wanted out of the auto racing business, Bill saw his chance and offered to take over the event and run the 1938 Daytona race. It turned out to be a success.

After that he expanded each year to locations in Georgia and the Carolinas and learned just what it took to make stock car racing a success. At the same time, other promoters were trying to do the same thing, but didn't have the France knack. France had the personality, the know-how, and the determined persistence to make stock car racing work. He even gave his expanded enterprise a name, the National Championship Stock Car Circuit (NCSCC).

The smart businessman inside of William France quickly recognized that car racing, which took place mostly in the South, was too disorganized and spotty for drivers to make a steady living at it. Beyond that, there was another serious problem in making money for himself and many of the others interested in racing—crooks. Hustlers were attracted to racing in those days because it was very loosely run. A lot of people came out to watch and spend money and a fast-talking, fast-moving con man could make money. For example, a promoter would organize a race at a dirt track, sign on a bunch of drivers and people to put on the race, sell lots of tickets, and disappear with the money.

After France had been in the business for nine years, he decided the honest operators had to create an association with a solid set of rules and enforce them in order to clean up the sport and push out the con men and crooks. He called trusted racing friends and colleagues to meet with him at the Streamline Hotel in Daytona Beach early in December 1947. They agreed on several basic ideas to make racing successful both as a sport and as a moneymaker. First of all, he understood that the big appeal of stock car racing was that it did not involve special racing cars removed from the personal experience of the fans. It used "stock" cars just like what the fans drove. So, to enhance that fantasy, France believed all the cars in the races had to be *new* stock cars. Fans didn't want to see a jalopy race, he said; they wanted to see the latest in stock cars.

Next, France insisted that cars be equal with one another in technical specifications. That meant the win would be largely a function of the driver, the human element. Finally, it was important that the hustlers be barred from racing, and that required a strong professional national organization to regulate the sport. That's how the National Association for Stock Car Automobile Racing

(NASCAR) got started. It was incorporated in February 1948 with William France as its president. He was its strongest promoter for years.

France clearly understood that NASCAR was not in the racing business and not in the car business. It was in the entertainment business, and if it wasn't fun for the paying customers, it wasn't going to work. So instead of beginning its first season in 1948 when NASCAR was born, France held off a year until 1949. He knew that many people in 1948 were still driving old, outdated family cars from before World War II and it wouldn't be fun for them to see brand-new models racing when orders were so backlogged that the average person couldn't get one. Bill waited until 1949 when everything was in order for his first NASCAR trial race, which took place on February 27 at Broward, Florida, and then set up the official opening race in Charlotte as a showcase of stock production-model car racing.

NASCAR also had to succeed as a business. France knew that the main money he needed to count on for the success of NASCAR would have to come from corporate sponsors, which was another reason he insisted on an honest operation. Corporate sponsors don't want to be affiliated with something crooked or slipshod, and France was going to ensure that they got good value for their sponsorship money. One of France's levers was to punish stock car drivers who raced in "outlaw" races, events not sanctioned by NASCAR. He would fine them or punish them with the ultimate threat—being banned from NASCAR.

The fans' reaction to NASCAR racing was immediate and very strong. They turned out by the thousands, and Bill France's concept was paying off for all the promoters who joined NASCAR and adhered to its rules and approach. Soon the concept of a superspeedway was introduced at Darlington, South Carolina, and the first Southern 500 was showcased there in 1950, before 25,000 enthusiastic fans. On the personal side, France would rebuild his Daytona track several years later into a superspeedway, making it one of the two premiere races of the NASCAR circuit.

France was a tough leader and determined to build this new sport by keeping it honest, safe, and fair. Developing along with NASCAR were a number of key drivers such as Lee Petty, Fred Lorenzen, David Pearson, Cale Yarborough, and Ned Jarrett, and supporting them were the car manufacturers who saw NASCAR as a prime promotion device for selling their cars. Early in the life of NASCAR, the American car manufacturers began to field racing teams and get heavily involved in the sport. It was all working according to Bill France's plan.

Bill France founded NASCAR with a vision that has sustained him, his family, and the organization from the beginning. He retired in 1972 and turned everything over to his son, Bill Jr.

In 1980, a man in Bristol, Connecticut, Bill Rasmussen, launched a twenty-four-hour all-sports cable television network and he called it Entertainment Sports Programming Network or ESPN. It was rough going at first because many sports clubs in football, baseball, basketball, and so on wanted to sell the TV rights to their games and ESPN didn't have the money to participate. So, initially, ESPN was showing a lot of spare events such as Canadian professional football that had a set of rules that most Americans didn't understand.

In the early 1980s ESPN was desperate for sporting events. William France Jr. bought into that situation and sold ESPN on making NASCAR racing a regular part of its programming. Up until then, the only NASCAR events on TV were the Daytona 500 and a handful of other events. Now ESPN would cover all the NASCAR races, and by 1995 it brought the events to more than sixty-four million homes.

Something else continues to work very well for NASCAR. Its stars mingle with the fans, give out autographs (free!), and are very involved in sponsor and fan events. This adds to the excitement of the sport. The result is that today almost six million fans attend races and millions more are watching at home. The watching at home, of course, is a plus for the racing team sponsors whose logos, painted on the NASCAR competition cars, are constantly flashing on millions of TV sets without costing the sponsors a dime in broadcast advertising.

The impact of TV on NASCAR racing was astonishing to many because it rocketed the motor sport to a major moneymaker, pulling in a $2 billion gross every year and paying out a third of a billion in prize money to make drivers and team owners wealthy. And now, years after NASCAR first went on TV for free, it is earning money from the TV people in addition to sponsorships, gate entrance fees, and sale of memorabilia. Other income sources include licensing the NASCAR name, the new NASCAR Thunder stores around the country, and the new NASCAR cafés.

NASCAR has changed its symbols as its audience has changed. It was, and still is, a sport almost entirely male and almost entirely white, but that is slowly changing. The new audience is national and its new symbol is Jeff Gordon. Jeff Gordon was adopted by the media, and the hook to its story was that he *wasn't* an ex-bootlegger from the hills of the South. He was just a clean-cut kid from the Midwest. Jeff Gordon is NASCAR's dream man because he is a sponsor's dream man. Today's NASCAR driver is a spokesman who spends a lot of time in direct contact with the public, his fans, and potential customers for his sponsor's product. Jeff is very telegenic and is an ideal package of talent, guts, charm, and good looks. The television camera is in love with him and that is just as valuable as his knowledge of how to use an opponent's back draft in a race.

Interestingly, Ray Evernham is also one of the new NASCAR breed. He is a hard-working, talented mechanic, organizer, and racing strategist, but he is very media-minded. He spends time giving speeches, appearing on radio and TV broadcasts, doing television features for The Nashville

Network (TNN), and, like Jeff, is an award winner. This is not the time of Mr. Greasy Overalls. This is the time of Mr. Pressed Uniform, always ready with a quote for the media. In the fall of 1996, Ray and Jeff were the featured speakers at a packed seminar for freshman engineering students at Princeton University. A new NASCAR era is under way.

10

The Private Life of Jeff and Brooke

Jeff and Brooke Gordon are famous because of their public connection with NASCAR racing and the fairy-tale nature of their romance and marriage. But when Jeff isn't at the track racing and Brooke isn't at the track watching, they have another life. It is more public than many of us have, but it is still their "other life." Here are some glimpses into that not completely private life—vignettes from the personal lives of Jeff and Brooke.

THE JEFF AND BROOKE ROMANCE

Brooke Sealey grew up in Winston-Salem and attended the University of North Carolina. Never a race fan, she wouldn't have met her future husband except for a friend who suggested she interview to be a Miss Winston. The job of a Miss Winston is to appear at Winston Cup events, congratulate the winners at Victory Lane, and generally promote Winston Cup activities.

Jeff Gordon won the first race Brooke Sealey ever saw in 1992 at the Twin 125 qualifying race at Charlotte. As Miss Winston, Brooke was not supposed to date drivers, but Jeff had already seen her picture and called several times for a date—without results. She refused to return his calls. When they finally met on Valentine's Day 1992, before the Charlotte race, she gave him some heart-shaped candies for good luck. Later she would give him the trophy for winning the race. She said, "He was so sweet—so down to earth. Actually, he was not down to earth. He was floating on a cloud."

"Rule or no rule, in Victory Lane we were winking at each other." Jeff persisted and talked with Brooke afterward, using their youth as an excuse. He joked that the two of them were the youngest people involved in the Charlotte race. He seemed a little nervous and Brooke found that charming. The two of them met again at a charity event and later at an autograph signing. By that time, they both decided they wanted to see more of each other in spite of the no-dating rule that applied for the year she would reign as a

Miss Winston. They agreed that they would start going out, and if they were discovered, they would stop immediately until her year was up.

They began dating in secret quite regularly, going to places that the NASCAR crowd didn't frequent. They avoided attention by ducking in and out of side entrances and meeting at odd times. In some ways this added to the excitement of their courtship and it soon became very serious. There was one problem—Jeff's mustache. Jeff had grown a pencil-thin mustache when he was fourteen (and enhanced it with an eyebrow pencil) so he would look older. He still had it when he started dating Brooke. After several months of dating, Brooke asked him if he would ever shave it. She thought he would look even cuter without the mustache. Later in the evening, Jeff left the table to go to the bathroom, and a few minutes later, he came back with the mustache shaved off to Brooke's surprise and delight. He's kept it off ever since.

Several times when they were together at restaurants, Brooke had to duck into kitchens and out back doors when other racers happened in. Once, as Jeff and Brooke were about to board a flight together, Darrell Waltrip's team arrived at the gate. She slipped away and had to wait two hours for another flight. As for race weekends, Jeff admits he was "a master at sneaking in and out of hotels." Immediately after they started dating, they had a scare. While waiting to get into a Hard Rock Cafe in Atlanta, race driver Kyle Petty spotted Jeff and almost discovered the identity of the woman with him. Luckily, Jeff was able to put Petty off, but it was a close call.

Some people wondered why Jeff Gordon always seemed to show up at racing social events alone. It got to the point that one driver challenged him directly at a party: "Look, you're young, you've got all this money, but you've never got any women around you. Are you gay?" The NASCAR crowd, a gossipy lot, buzzed all season about the handsome young driver who should have been a magnet for women but never seemed to have a date. They also wondered why Brooke Sealey didn't have a boyfriend and didn't bring dates to social functions. Yet the gossips never seemed to link the two juiciest items of the season. Both Jeff and Brooke were happy when her year as Miss Winston was over at the end of the 1993 season.

At the NASCAR Awards Banquet in New York that December, Jeff Gordon was honored as Rookie of the Year, with record first-

year winnings of $765,000, and Brooke
Sealey's season as Miss Winston officially
ended. The two finally revealed their romance and left the gossips gaping. At Daytona the following February, the day before
the Busch Clash, and a year to the day
from the couple's Victory Lane encounter of
1993, there came the night of the Big Question. There are conflicting stories about
exactly what happened. Everybody agrees
that it took place at a fancy French restaurant. Some say Gordon reserved a huge private room at a French restaurant and
Brooke was baffled when just the two of
them were seated. Others say there was a
Unocal party in progress in the restaurant
with a lot of racing types hanging around the
place and Gordon stalled because he didn't
want to propose while they were around.
Whichever story is right, both end when he
finally proposed and Brooke accepted
instantly. The next day he won the Busch
Clash and, soon after, he won his first Winston Cup race at Charlotte. It was a triple-
slam for Jeff.

Brooke, incidentally, in addition to being
Miss Winston in 1993, achieved a number of
things on her own before she met Jeff. She is
a licensed insurance agent in North Carolina,
where she was born and raised. She majored

in psychology at the University of North Carolina and was a member of the Chi Omega sorority. A model for Marilyn's Modeling Agency in Greensboro, Brooke has worked on Hanes, Chiquita, and Sony accounts in addition to being a spokesperson for Pepsi-Cola.

Most Jeff Gordon fans were excited about the wedding of Jeff and Brooke, but naturally it was not possible for all of them to attend. The Gordons and Sealeys wanted to keep it a family affair, but they did arrange for fans to send in drawings or letters and these were bound into congratulations books for the couple. Fans were also able to mark the wedding with a donation to the Leukemia Society of America, Jeff's favorite charity since his crew chief's son, Ray Evernham Jr., is a recovering victim of that disease.

They were married in Charlotte on November 26, 1994, in an elaborate ceremony that included a Founders Hall reception, a seven-foot-high wedding cake, and a cover shot on *Carolina Bride* magazine. They bought a home alongside Lake Norman in the outskirts of Charlotte. (Some people think of it as Lake Speed because it is home to many race drivers and people in the world of motor sports racing.) The two have been apart for only two days since they were married.

Brooke travels with Jeff everywhere. They are pictured together so often in part because they rarely leave each other's side once he pulls himself out of his race car.

All of this has had a good effect on Jeff's life and his career. From the personal-life standpoint, Gordon says, "I'm so happy with my life now. I'm not out searching anymore. Brooke has brought so much joy into my life."

From the career side of things it has also made the lives of the Rainbow Warriors easier, too, as Ray Evernham reports that Brooke brought a major change in Gordon. Ray said, "Since he's been married to Brooke he's a totally different person. He's more patient. I think she has really helped his driving."

Jeff and Brooke live in a spacious, four-bedroom mansion and keep busy with their various "toys," which include a forty-five-foot motor home, a Lear jet, a twenty-nine-foot speedboat, and a red Jaguar XK-8.

OFF-TRACK RECREATION

The hand-eye coordination necessary to be a winner on the track has also made Jeff a winner in less stressful situations, namely, playing video games and pinball. He has been known, for example, to go up against some of his fans in video race games—and wins almost all the time. His public relations manager, Ron Miller, says Jeff has spent his life driving a race car and that also makes him good at video games. "Don't ever challenge him at video games. You'll lose. He's very, very good." Jeff is so good, his friends joke that when he goes to a public arcade, he makes all the kids cry. But there are limits to fun and Jeff has learned what some of them are. For example, when he jumped at the chance to fly with the famous Blue Angels, he lost his lunch. Asked if he'd do it again, he says, "Absolutely not."

Jeff and Brooke spend a lot of their free time together, playing basketball at home, going out on their Sea-Doos for some watersports fun, and sometimes playing a little golf. Movies are great for the Gordons in that they don't run into many race fans there and they can enjoy some private recreation. They go to the movies so much that their friends kid them by calling them "Siskel and Ebert." Jeff does admit that he suffers terribly from allergies to, he says, "everything that grows outdoors." Brooke teases him that it's just his way of getting out of mowing the lawn.

Jeff loves Edy's rocky road ice cream. Actually, rocky road is probably *the* favorite thing in Jeff's life after Brooke and the Victory Lane! The two of them frequently stay home to watch TV; *Seinfeld* and *Melrose Place* are their two favorites. His lucky number is six, his golf score is usually around one hundred, and he admits that he doesn't think ahead too much. He tends to focus on the immediate to the point that, he says, "I usually don't know what I'm doing this afternoon." His favorite clothes are jeans, a knit shirt, and Nikes.

JEFF AND BROOKE'S CHRISTIAN FAITH

Neither Jeff nor Brooke make big public displays about their faith, but they are both active and devoted Christians, and that was largely Brooke's doing and inspiration.

Jeff credits Brooke with having a wonderful heart and being the one who has brought out the good in him. He says that, given his lifestyle and the temptations it brings, he easily could have turned the wrong way, but he didn't because Brooke taught him to be focused by bringing Christ into their lives and home. Jeff is pleased with his commitment to Christ and says that if he ran into any of his friends today from five years ago, they wouldn't recognize him anymore. Jeff and Brooke regularly attend church and Brooke can be seen praying for him at the start of every race. She has given him a special scripture, Proverbs 3:5–6, to help him and protect him that he often has in the car with him: "Trust in the Lord with all thine heart; and lean not unto thine own understanding. In all thy ways acknowledge Him and He shall direct thy paths."

Jeff's Christian involvement goes beyond attending church with Brooke. Recently Jeff has become a public witness giving speeches at mass rallies for Promise Keepers, a program that revolves around what its supporters perceive is God's plan for a husband: men are "to build strong marriages and families through love, protection, and biblical values." Many women, like Brooke, who support the program, see it bolstering men who love God to also love their wives and family.

Promise Keepers was started in Boulder, Colorado, in 1990 by Bill McCartney. He resigned from his position as the football coach at the University of Colorado to work filling stadiums with men cheering for something beyond football and stock car races. The objective of Promise Keepers is to sell men on the idea that it is manly to read the Bible, pray, attend church, raise their children, and be loyal to their wives. On October 4, 1997, it staged its biggest gathering yet on the Mall in Washington, D.C., with several hundred thousand in attendance.

In addition, Jeff is active in several charities, such as the Leukemia Society (inspired by the tragedies of his team owner and his crew chief's son), Kids and the Hood, and the Make-A-Wish Foundation.

JEFF AND HIS FANS

The big thing that makes Jeff such a successful and famous driver is that he is more than just an exceptional race car driver. Jeff, Brooke, and their staff are very savvy about what has to be done off the track to keep those stands filled and those souvenirs selling. Jeff is ideal for this kind of quasi-public, quasi-private life and he has more appeal than most people in his field. For example, although he has been a professional for less than five years, he goes out of his way to be accessible to his fans. This is not true of all race car drivers and even less true in other professional sports. Jeff knows who pays the money at the gate, who cheers him from the stands, and who is buying millions of dollars of Jeff Gordon souvenirs. And so does Brooke, who is with him most of the time.

Jeff is talented on the track, but he also has those all-American good looks and knows how to respond to his thousands of fans. He has been on the David Letterman and Jay Leno shows several times; he has a growing fan club with fifteen thousand enthusiastic members and a very popular Web site on the Internet; and he is constantly charming women fans into watching his sport. John Krol, the CEO of DuPont, Jeff's racing sponsor, wouldn't dare not sponsor Jeff Gordon because one of Jeff's biggest fans is Krol's mother-in-law! "She's eighty-three, she's never even had a driver's license, and she watches every race!"

Tennis star and friend Monica Seles says Jeff works harder at being with and pleasing his fans off the track than any other athlete she knows. He is with them on race days, talking, shaking hands, and signing autographs.

11

The Future of NASCAR and Jeff Gordon

Jeff Gordon is seen as the catalyst who will propel his sport into the twenty-first century. He is NASCAR's premiere rising star. Humpy Wheeler, president of the Charlotte Motor Speedway, calls it straight and plain: "He gives stock car racing a real shot in the arm, especially for the eighteen-to-twenty-five age group. People like youth. They like something new. We all needed a Jeff Gordon."

Gordon's smart, aggressive driving on the track has male fans yelling for him, but he also has a softer side that has women fans supporting him, too. He is still a little boy in some ways with a starstruck innocence and awe at meeting other celebrities, and that appeals to female fans. Every one of them knows Jeff saved a little box of candy hearts, the kind that read "Kiss Me" and "Be Mine," that Brooke gave him one Valentine's Day. And he even admits to being emotional. He loves racing, is excited about it, and effervescent when he wins and depressed when he loses. He set the tone with his first win in the Winston Cup circuit. "I'm not ashamed to say I bawled my eyes out when I won the 600 in Charlotte," he says. "My lip started shaking with ten laps to go." And when he won the first Brickyard 400 he told bystanders that he was like a kid in a candy store.

Gregarious and socially smooth, he makes corporate public relations people giddy watching him work a cocktail party regaling the guests with stories about the night he and Brooke lost their cat for three hours or giving everybody his abbreviated movie reviews. "He's a sponsor's dream," says Rick Hendrick. There is also praise from his toughest competition, leading NASCAR driver Dale Earnhardt. "He's the best young talent that's ever been out there."

As for the future, Gordon sees many years ahead with NASCAR in his life. "I'm counting on a long career," says Gordon, "and stock car racing is where I want to be." That's all possible because many of the contemporary NASCAR drivers are almost twice Jeff's age.

NASCAR is in the midst of a major transition as it approaches the twenty-first century. With a new configuration of sponsors, fans, and drivers, NASCAR is moving to make itself a family-oriented glamour sport featuring articulate, handsome stars. Jeff Gordon is its poster boy.

In his book *Wheels,* author Paul Hemphill summarized the situation when he noted that the marquee value of the older drivers over the age of forty and fifty is not very high. Most of them had not won a Winston Cup race in a good while and very few fans even knew who they are. Hemphill draws an analogy to the Grand Ole Opry, where a singer becomes a "regular" on the basis of one song and then keeps showing up on-stage for years afterward. Both NASCAR and the Grand Ole Opry got stuck by guaranteeing these old-timers a spot on the menu for every major event. Of course the old favorites still draw big fan responses—for example, Rusty Wallace, Terry Labonte, Dale Jarrett, and the driver Jeff Gordon says he tries to emulate, Mark Martin. Any one of these men can drive a mean race on a given weekend, but none of them is a fresh, new talent in his twenties.

The people who run NASCAR and the various racing teams for whom this sport is big business know they have to have the heroes to attract the audiences that, in turn, attract the sponsors and TV—all of which brings in the money. NASCAR is on TV every week, and it needs the matinee-idol hero other sports have to attract and hold audiences. So the sudden emergence of Jeff Gordon with his skill and his style was a huge blessing. He is the mark of the future for NASCAR, and most of those on the business side of the sport know it.

In his short time as part of NASCAR's elite Winston Cup circuit, the youthful Gordon has accomplished more than many veterans have achieved in a lifetime of fender-banging. Gordon is the greatest talent to hit the NASCAR track since Dale Earnhardt emerged twenty years ago. The difference is that it was all a struggle for Earnhardt, while Gordon seems to have glided in on the wings of good fortune.

Earnhardt's rougher road has given him nicknames such as The Intimidator, The Dominator, The Terminator, The Man in Black. These names echo his philosophy of winning at any cost. Earnhardt is notorious for flooring his Black Chevrolet Number 3 and nudging, bumping, pushing, and forcing into the wall anybody in his way. For him there are only two positions at the end of the race, either winner or loser. If you're first, you're the winner; if you're not, you're the loser no matter where you finished. Typical of his tough demeanor, he was once criticized for failing to obey a black flag signal to stop because his car was leaking oil and endangering other drivers. Earnhardt flipped back, "I wasn't looking for the black. I was looking for the checkered." All of this coupled with his acknowledged superior skill is the reason he is regarded by many as the best NASCAR driver ever to grace a track—except, of course, at the Daytona 500, which he has never won.

So, by comparison, just how good can Jeff be? Benny Parsons, the 1973 Winston Cup champion and ESPN analyst, says, "It's difficult to imagine Jeff being any better than he is now. But, of course, he will improve with experience, and that's awesome to picture."

THE LAST LAP

Here we end our story, temporarily, but this ending is only the beginning for Jeff and for the new NASCAR of the future. In December 1997, NASCAR celebrated its fiftieth anniversary and it has been a fascinating half century since Bill France and thirty-five mechanics, drivers, and racing promoters met at the Streamline Hotel in Daytona Beach and founded NASCAR.

Jeff Gordon's emergence on the NASCAR national scene in the 1990s was like a breath of fresh air for stock car racing. The natural born winner will be in the driver's seat as NASCAR begins its next fifty years. Get ready for the ride of your life!

APPENDIX

Jeff Gordon
at a Glance

Hometown: Pittsboro, Indiana
Residence: Huntersville, North Carolina
Birthdate: August 4, 1971, in Vallejo,
   California
Wife: Brooke (née Sealey)
Height: 5′ 7″
Weight: 150
Hobbies: Golf, water skiing, and video
   games
Race car: Chevrolet Monte Carlo
Personal vehicle: Chevrolet Blazer
Address: c/o Hendrick Motorsports, P.O. Box
   9, Harrisburg, NC 28075

JEFF'S CUMULATIVE NASCAR RACING RECORD

	Races	Wins	Top 5	Top 10	Winnings
1992	1	0	0	0	$6,285
1993	30	0	7	11	765,168
1994	31	2	7	14	1,779,523
1995	31	7	10	16	4,347,343
1996	31	10	21	24	3,428,485
1997	32	10	22	23	4,089,042

Years Racing	Total Races	Total Wins	Total Top 5s	Total Top 10s	Total Winnings
6	153	29	66	87	$14,415,846

Jeff Gordon/Kellogg's National Fan Club

P.O. Box 515, Williams, AZ 86046-0515
(520) 635-JEFF
Fax: (520) 635-2583
E-mail: jgfan@primenet.com
Web site: www.jeffgordonfanclub.com

NASCAR fans love Gordon. His fan club numbers more than thirty thousand; his souvenir sales rank second on the circuit, just behind Earnhardt and well ahead of Rusty Wallace. He gets fifty requests a week for interviews, twenty more for personal appearances. Jeff has an active international fan club, the Jeff Gordon/Kellogg's National Fan Club headquartered in Williams, Arizona, which merchandises Jeff Gordon mementos, promotes his races and career, and issues a monthly newsletter about Jeff, his life, and activities involving him.

Typical of the campaigns the fan club

runs to promote Jeff is the one to make Jeff the NASCAR Winston Cup Most Popular Driver. The voting is by telephone call and the fan club advises members to call between July 15 and November 18. Each fan is allowed ten calls per day with a maximum of twenty-five calls in all. The number from which the call is placed is checked and it doesn't take a genius to figure out one can make as many calls as one wants to make as long as no more than twenty-five originate from the same number. Naturally, somebody is making money off of these calls to 1-900-903-0909 at the rate of seventy-nine cents per call.

The fan club is organized into regions with an organization coordinator for each who plans and runs various events including guest appearances by Jeff Gordon. Examples of recent meetings range from a $15 Charlotte fan club meeting serving snacks, which sold out with 250 attendees, to a special Atlanta Motorspeedway VIP-suite three-day meeting at $550 per person, which also sold out. All the clubs schedule a meeting the night of the Winston Cup awards. The fan club also sells tickets to various races and Jeff Gordon appearances along with a dizzying array of Jeff Gordon memorabilia. The newsletter lists items from trading cards to hats to shirts to pins to infant bibs to autographed pictures to bumper stickers to 1/64 model cars to earrings to flags to dog leashes to suspenders to shoelaces to notepads to clutch purses.

The club is divided into ten regions, with the first eight covering the U.S., the ninth consisting of Canada, and the tenth including the U.S. military overseas and the rest of the world.

Not fully appreciated by those who are not stock car fans is the symbolism and profit involved in the nonracing part of NASCAR. At every Winston Cup race there is a row of souvenir stands selling everything from clothing to toys to food to bumper stickers to earrings to hats to kid and baby stuff, all with the picture or name of a racing hero on them. As one observer said after mixing with the thousands of people milling around these stands, "This is not a place for the faint of heart or faint of credit card." The average fan spends over $200 on souvenirs at a race, and Dale Earnhardt may be the king of the souvenir game. *U.S. News and World Report* checked out the take on his souvenir business in 1996 and concluded that Earnhardt, through a company called Sports Image, sells some five thousand T-shirts at every Winston Cup event for $20 each, a total take of $3.1 million a year on T-shirts alone! The total souvenir gross for Earnhardt is estimated at $42 million a year, from which, of course, one has to deduct the cost of making and selling these items, but it is still a tidy income. Visiting souvenir row or reading the Jeff Gordon Fan Club newsletter, where much of the space is devoted to selling souvenirs, shows that Jeff Gordon's line of souvenirs is in that same range.

Fan club membership costs $19.95 for an individual for one year, or $24.95 for a one-year, two-person family membership. Each member receives a welcoming packet with a postcard and other items about Jeff. In addition, members get a membership card and certificate, a 10 percent discount on some merchandise sold at the track, and twelve issues of the Jeff Gordon Fan Club newsletter. Family members also receive a copy of the Jeff Gordon handbook and his Winston Cup statistics.

The fan club, which now has approximately 15,000 members, is organized into ten regions with a coordinator for each region.

Region #1
Brenda Demos: 3702 North Lake Boulevard, Danville, IL 61832; (217) 443-4210
   Illinois
   Indiana
   Iowa
   Michigan
   Minnesota
   Missouri
   Ohio
   Wisconsin

Region #2
Kevin Methven: 2-D Washington Drive, West Paterson, NJ 07424; (201) 785-8873; E-mail kevin3735@aol.com
   Connecticut
   Delaware
   Maine
   Maryland
   Massachusetts
   New Hampshire
   New Jersey
   New York
   Pennsylvania
   Rhode Island
   Vermont

Region #3
Anthony Plante: 1409 Cardinal Drive, West

Columbia, SC 29169; (803) 739-7054; E-mail
arplante@aol.com
  Kentucky
  North Carolina
  South Carolina
  Tennessee
  Virginia
  West Virginia

Region #4
Kim Miller: 509 Chitwood, Kennedale, TX
76060; (817) 679-4194; E-mail klm3917@acs.
tamu.edu
  Arkansas
  Louisiana
  Oklahoma
  Texas

Region #5
Sandy Champlin: 1279 Avenida Floribunda,
San Jacinto, CA 92583; (909) 487-8735;
E-mail schampl@pe.net
  Arizona
  California (southern)
  Hawaii
  New Mexico

Region #6
Joe Klingensmith: 656 Benicia Road, Vallejo,
CA 94591; (707) 552-2916
  Alaska

California (northern)
Idaho
Nevada
Oregon
Washington

Region #7
Clay Stanley: 13251 Brookside Drive, Bellevue, NE 68123; (402) 293-5945
Colorado
Kansas
Montana
Nebraska
North Dakota
South Dakota
Utah
Wyoming

Region #8
Michelle Alonso: 7402 North Springs Drive, Acworth, GA 30101; (770) 917-9420
Alabama
Florida
Georgia
Mississippi
Puerto Rico

Region #9
Gary Laver: 27 Birchfield Court, Courtice, Ontario, Canada L1E 1M4; (905) 432-3681
Canada

Region #10
Gusti Hiemeyer: Sauerlacherstr. 62, 82515
Wolfratshausen, Germany; (08171) 29777;
Fax (08171) 16407
   Military overseas and foreign countries

COLLECTIBLES BUSINESS

   Much of the fan club's newsletters are
devoted to souvenir items and collectibles
and a regular column is written for the
newsletters about them by Paul Rideout
#093 at P.O. Box 852, Bristol, CT 06011.

T-shirts
Shorts
Sweatshirts and pants
Golf and polo shirts
Jackets
Hats
Accessories
   Seat cushion
   Hat pin
   Button
   Car magnet
   Car decal
   Hair bow
   Ladies socks
   Shot glass

Shooter glass
Coffee mug
Key chain
License plate frame
Earrings
Charm
Sunglasses
Flag
Beach towel
Yo-yo
Wristwatch
Glo-watch

Pictures

Collection Items

12-Card Set
Carolina Bride magazine
NASCAR pocket planner
Set of 10 postcards
Maxx race cards (20)
Silver medallion
Racing fantasy book
Telephone calling card
NASCAR calendar
Activity and coloring books
Die-cast car
Prior newsletters

NASCAR Words

Here is what many of the technical words used around the NASCAR circuit mean:

Alabama Gang   A group of NASCAR drivers who all come from a small town in Alabama by the name of Hueytown. Some of the drivers in the Alabama Gang are Davey and Cliff Allison and Neil Bonnett, who are now dead, and Bobby and Donnie Allison, who are alive, along with Hut Stricklin and Red Farmer.

Bootlegger's Turn   A complete U-turn to run from a police road block. Usually done by crimping the steering wheel hard to the left or right and tromping on the gas at the same time to spin the car around and head in the opposite direction. Rarely seen these days outside of reruns of the TV series *The Dukes of Hazzard*.

Brake Fade   Sometimes during racing, the

brake fluid will get so hot that it boils releasing air into the brake lines. When this happens and the driver pushes down on the brake pedal, it goes to the floor and he can't stop the car.

Busch Grand National   Racing circuit that is one level lower than the championship Winston Cup Series.

CART   Acronym for Championship Auto Racing Teams

Craftsman Truck Series   A third NASCAR circuit, besides Busch Grand National and Winston Cup, with pickup truck bodies mounted on stock car chassis created to appeal to the growing number of truck owners in America.

Flags   Flags are used by NASCAR officials to notify drivers of some important information while they are on the track racing. See the following section for an explanation of the flag signals.

Formula One   A mostly European racing sport involving vehicles using the latest technology (as opposed to the "stock car" concept). Races are held at locations worldwide but the one through the streets of Monte Carlo is the best known.

Fuel Cell   A mandatory container for carrying fuel in all NASCAR cars. It is a twenty-two-gallon bladder in a metal tank that prevents gasoline from spilling out in an accident.

Go-Kart Inexpensive, low-powered racer mostly raced by young people. Comes in many sizes and variations.

IRL Acronym for the Indy Racing League, which was started in 1995 by the president of the Indianapolis Motor Speedway, Tony George. It is designed to compete with CART.

Modified A NASCAR-approved car that has been altered from the usual, car-dealer showroom model. Changes are approved to make them safer or handle better.

Pole The number one starting position in a race. It is the inside, first-row spot at the start and goes to whoever has won the qualifying race. So to "win a pole" means to have won a qualifying race. In 1998, before the beginning of the season and the Daytona 500 in February, all the pole winners will race February 8 at a non-championship points event (a just-for-fun race) called the Budweiser Shootout. The official opening race of the season, the Daytona 500, comes a week later on February 15.

Oversteer A condition, also called being "loose," where the car doesn't respond well to the driver's steering. When the driver turns the wheel, the car will swing too far and he is in danger of spinning out.

Rear Spoiler A blade mounted on the rear deck lid of the car designed to alter the air turbulence sweeping over the car. By adjusting the vertical angle of the spoiler, the driver and crew can change the downward air pressure that is applied to the car by the air turbulence. This has a major effect on how the car handles.

Restrictor Plate A plate attached between the carburetor and the air intake that, as the name says, restricts the amount of air to the engine and reduces the power of the engine. This is used only at the two superspeedway tracks, Daytona and Talladega.

Setup All the various adjustments made to the car's engine, aerodynamics (such as the rear spoiler), tires, brakes, etc., for racing that particular day at that particular track.

Stagger Use of different-size tires on different wheels to make the car handle better in the race. For example, at the usual track where the cars turn only to the left, mounting slightly larger tires on the two right wheels gives the car more traction on the right side when turning left.

What Do All Those Flags Mean?

Black   Pull into your pit; you have broken one of the racing rules. This is used to signal an individual driver.

Black-and-White Crossed   You are no longer being scored because you have not obeyed the black flag signal. This is used to signal individual drivers that, essentially, they are out of the race.

Blue with Yellow Lines   Move over and let faster cars pass you. This is given to drivers who are going too slow and are holding up the race.

Checkered   The end of the race. This is the flag every driver has been looking for during the several hours of the race.

Green   The starting flag and signal to begin the race or, if it was interrupted, to resume the race.

Red   Everybody stop. The race is halted,

often because of weather or a bad accident.

White There is only one lap to go in the race.

Yellow Be careful; something is wrong on the track. This could be an accident, wreckage, oil on the track, or rain.

1998 Winston Cup Racing Schedule

(Subject to Change)

Sunday	February 8	Bud Shootout, Daytona Speedway*
Sunday	February 15	Daytona 500, Daytona Speedway (Official Season Opener)
Sunday	February 22	North Carolina Motor Speedway
Sunday	March 1	Las Vegas Motor Speedway
Sunday	March 8	Atlanta Motor Speedway
Sunday	March 22	Darlington Raceway
Sunday	March 29	Bristol Motor Speedway

Sunday	April 5	Texas Motor Speedway
Sunday	April 19	Martinsville Speedway
Sunday	April 26	Talladega Superspeedway
Sunday	May 3	California Speedway
Saturday	May 16	The Winston— Charlotte Motor Speedway*
Sunday	May 24	Charlotte Motor Speedway
Sunday	May 31	Dover Downs International Speedway
Saturday	June 6	Richmond International Speedway
Sunday	June 14	Michigan Speedway
Sunday	June 21	Pocono Speedway
Sunday	June 28	Sears Point Raceway
Saturday	July 4	Daytona International Speedway
Sunday	July 12	New Hampshire

		International Speedway
Sunday	July 26	Pocono Raceway
Saturday	August 1	Indianapolis Motor Speedway
Sunday	August 9	Watkins Glen International
Sunday	August 16	Michigan Speedway
Saturday	August 22	Bristol Motor Speedway
Sunday	August 30	New Hampshire International Speedway
Sunday	September 6	Darlington Raceway
Saturday	September 12	Richmond International Raceway
Sunday	September 20	Dover Downs International Speedway
Sunday	September 27	Martinsville Speedway
Sunday	October 4	Charlotte Motor Speedway
Sunday	October 11	Talladega Superspeedway
Sunday	October 25	North Carolina Motor Speedway

Sunday	November 1	Phoenix International Raceway
Sunday	November 8	Atlanta Motor Speedway (End of Winston Cup Season)
Sunday	November 15	Suzuka Circuit, Japan*
Saturday	November 21	Twin Ring Motegi, Japan*

*Nonpoints race

Jeff Gordon Racing Results, 1994–1997

1994 WINSTON CUP SEASON
(Races won by Jeff Gordon are in bold)

		Start/Finish Position
February 13	**Busch Clash of '94, Daytona** (Nonpoints)	6/1
February 20	Daytona 500, Daytona Beach, FL	6/4
February 27	Goodwrench 500, Rockingham, NC	3/32
March 6	Pontiac Excitement 400, Richmond, VA	8/3
March 13	Purolator 500, Atlanta, GA	17/8
March 27	TranSouth Financial 400, Darlington, NC	13/31

April 10	Food City 500, Bristol, TN	4/22
April 17	First Union 400, North Wilkesboro, NC	12/15
April 24	Hanes 500, Martinsville, VA	13/33
May 1	Winston Select 500, Talladega, AL	40/24
May 15	Save Mart Supermarkets 300, Sonoma, CA	6/37
May 21	Winston Select All-Star, Charlotte, NC (Nonpoints)	15/14
May 29	**Coca-Cola 600, Concord, NC**	**1/1**
June 5	Budweiser 500, Dover, DE	23/5
June 12	Pocono 500, Pocono, PA	4/6
June 19	Miller Genuine Draft 400, Brooklyn, MI	7/12
July 2	Pepsi 400, Daytona Beach, FL	12/8
July 10	Slick 50 300, Loudon, NH	2/39
July 17	Miller Genuine Draft 500, Pocono, PA	7/8
July 24	Die-Hard 500, Talladega, AL	15/31

August 6	**Inaugural Brickyard 400, Indianapolis, IN**	**3/1**
August 14	The Bud at the Glen, Watkins Glen, NY	3/9
August 21	GM Goodwrench Dealer 400, Brooklyn, MI	3/15
August 27	Goody's 500, Bristol, TN	12/32
September 4	Mountain Dew Southern 500, Darlington, SC	7/6
September 10	Miller Genuine Draft 400, Richmond, VA	13/2
September 18	Splitfire Spark Plug, Dover, DE	12/11
September 25	Goody's 500, Martinsville, VA	6/11
October 2	Tyson Holly Farms 400, North Wilkesboro, NC	12/8
October 9	Mello Yello, Charlotte, NC	5/28
October 23	AC-Delco 400, Rockingham, NC	15/29
October 30	Slick 50 500, Phoenix, AZ	14/4
November 13	Hooters 500, Atlanta, GA	6/15

1995 WINSTON CUP SEASON
(Races won by Jeff Gordon are in bold)

		Start/Finish Position
February 19	Daytona 500, Daytona Beach, FL	4/22
February 26	**Goodwrench 500, Rockingham, NC**	**1/1**
March 5	Pontiac Excitement 400, Richmond, VA	1/36
March 12	**Purolator 500, Hampton, GA**	**3/1**
March 26	TranSouth Financial 400, Darlington, NC	1/32
April 2	**Food City 500, Bristol, TN**	**2/1**
April 9	First Union 400, North Wilkesboro, NC	1/2
April 23	Hanes 500, Martinsville, VA	12/3
April 30	Winston Select 500, Talladega, AL	6/2
May 7	Save Mart Supermarkets 300, Sonoma, CA	5/3
May 20	**Winston Select All-Star, Concord, NC (Nonpoints)**	**7/1**

May 28	Coca-Cola 600, Concord, NC	1/33
June 4	Dover 500, Dover, DE	1/6
June 11	UAW-GM Teamwork 500, Long Pond, PA	5/16
June 18	Miller Genuine Draft 400, Brooklyn, MI	1/2
July 1	**Pepsi 400, Daytona Beach, FL**	**3/1**
July 9	**Slick 50 300, Loudon, NH**	**21/1**
July 16	Miller Genuine Draft 500, Long Pond, PA	11/2
July 23	Die-Hard 500, Talladega, AL	3/8
August 5	Brickyard 400, Indianapolis, IN	1/6
August 13	The Bud at the Glen, Watkins Glen, NY	5/3
August 20	The GM Goodwrench Dealer 400, Brooklyn, MI	21/3
August 26	Goody's 500, Bristol, TN	4/6
September 3	**Mountain Dew Southern 500, Darlington, SC**	**5/1**
September 9	Miller Genuine Draft 400, Richmond, VA	2/6
September 17	**MBNA 500, Dover, DE**	**2/1**
September 24	Goody's 500, Martinsville, VA	1/7

October 1	Tyson Holly Farms 400, North Wilkesboro, NC	14/3
October 8	UAW-GM 500, Concord, NC	3/30
October 22	AC-Delco 400, Rockingham, NC	4/20
October 29	Slick 50 500, Phoenix, AZ	3/5
November 12	NAPA 500, Hampton, GA	8/32

1996 WINSTON CUP SEASON
(Races won by Jeff Gordon are in bold)

		Start/Finish Position
February 18	Daytona 500, Daytona Beach, FL	8/42
February 25	Goodwrench 500, Rockingham, NC	2/40
March 3	**Pontiac Excitement 400, Richmond, VA**	**2/1**
March 10	Purolator 500, Hampton, GA	21/3
March 24	**TranSouth Financial 400, Darlington, SC**	**2/1**
March 31	**Food City 500, Bristol, TN**	**8/1**
April 14	First Union 400, North Wilkesboro, NC	17/2

April 21	Goody's 500, Martinsville, VA	13/3
April 28	Winston Select 500, Talladega, AL	11/33
May 5	Save Mart Supermarkets 300, Sonoma, CA	6/6
May 26	Coca-Cola 600, Concord, NC	1/4
June 2	**Dover 500, Dover, DE**	**1/1**
June 16	**UAW-GM Teamwork 500, Long Pond, PA**	**1/1**
June 23	Miller Genuine Draft 400, Brooklyn, MI	7/6
July 6	Pepsi 400, Daytona Beach, FL	1/3
July 14	Slick 50 300, Loudon, NH	16/34
July 21	Miller Genuine Draft 500, Long Pond, PA	15/7
July 28	**Die-Hard 500, Talladega, AL**	**2/1**
August 3	Brickyard 400, Speedway, IN	1/37
August 11	The Bud at the Glen, Watkins Glen, NY	5/4
August 18	GM Goodwrench Dealer 400, Brooklyn, MI	7/5
August 24	Goody's Headache 500, Bristol, TN	2/2

September 1	**Mountain Dew Southern 500, Darlington, SC**	**2/1**
September 7	Miller Genuine Draft 400, Richmond, VA	2/2
September 15	**MBNA 500, Dover, DE**	**3/1**
September 22	**Goody's Headache 500, Martinsville, VA**	**10/1**
September 29	**Tyson Holly Farms 400, North Wilkesboro, NC**	**2/1**
October 6	UAW-GM Quality 500, Concord, NC	2/31
October 20	AC-Delco 400, Rockingham, NC	3/12
October 27	Slick 50 500, Phoenix, AZ	19/5
November 10	NAPA, Atlanta, GA	2/3

1997 WINSTON CUP SEASON
(Races won by Jeff Gordon are in bold)

		Start/Finish Position
February 16	**Daytona 500, Daytona Beach, FL**	**6/1**
February 23	**Goodwrench Service 400, Rockingham, NC**	**4/1**
March 2	Pontiac Excitement 400, Richmond, VA	2/4

March 9	Primestar 500, Hampton, VA	23/42
March 23	TranSouth Financial 400, Darlington, SC	10/3
April 6	Interstate Batteries 500, Roanoke, TX	2/30
April 13	**Food City 500, Bristol, TN**	**5/1**
April 20	**Goody's Headache Powder 500, Martinsville, VA**	**4/1**
May 4	Save Mart Supermarkets 300, Sonoma, CA	3/2
May 10	Winston 500, Talladega, AL	11/5
May 25	**Coca-Cola 600, Concord, NC**	**1/1**
June 1	Miller 500, Dover, DE	2/26
June 8	**Pocono 500, Long Pond, PA**	**11/1**
June 15	Miller 400, Brooklyn, MI	12/5
June 22	**California 500 by NAPA, Fontana, CA**	**3/1**
July 5	Pepsi 400, Daytona Beach, FL	4/21
July 13	Jiffy Lube 300, Loudon, NH	29/23
July 20	Pennsylvania 500, Long Pond, PA	6/2

August 2	Brickyard 400, Indy Speedway, IN	24/4
August 10	**The Bud at the Glen, Watkins Glen, NY**	**11/1**
August 17	ITW Devilbiss 400, Brooklyn, MI	17/2
August 23	Goody's Headache Powder 500, Bristol, TN	2/35
August 31	**Mountain Dew Southern 500, Darlington, NC (The Million-Dollar Win for Jeff!)**	**7/1**
September 9	Exide Batteries Select 400, Richmond, VA	10/3
September 14	**CMT 300, Loudon, NH**	**13/1**
September 21	MBNA 400, Dover, DE	2/7
September 28	Hanes 500, Martinsville, VA	11/4
October 5	UAW-GM Quality 500, Concord, NC	4/5
October 12	Sears Die-Hard 500, Talladega, AL	8/35
October 27	AC-Delco 400, Rockingham, NC	4/4
November 2	Dura-Lube 500, Avondale, AZ	12/17
November 16	NAPA 500, Hampton, GA	37/17

WIDE OPEN
Days and Nights on the NASCAR Tour

By Shaun Assael

Published by Ballantine Books.
Available everywhere books are sold.

In WIDE OPEN, Shaun Assael takes us behind the scenes, into the pits, and onto the tracks, chronicling the days and nights of America's fastest-growing sport . . . a world of split-second life-or-death decisions . . . a megamoney world of big-city sports . . . a dramatic journey inside NASCAR's Winston Cup Tour.

Read on for a thrilling excerpt from
WIDE OPEN.

Introduction
"I GOT A FIRE"

Daytona: February 5–17, 1996

The Daytona International Speedway is quiet when the caravan of trailers starts arriving. Without people to bother them, seagulls nest in the infield grass. The air is clean; the overpowering smell of seared rubber hasn't yet settled in. There are no low-hanging clouds, mixing car exhaust with the smoke from a thousand greasy grills.

The arrival of the eighteen-wheelers, in a carnival of color-drenched logos, marks the unofficial start of the season. For the next eleven months they'll be traveling around the country together like a giant medicine revival, selling speed as the salvation for all that ails. Unlike other sports, which put down roots in a place, then live there over long seasons, the speed people don't stay in one place for long. Every week they're somewhere else, trying to solve the mystery of how to bleed two-hundredths of a second more out of a car. These are the increments that obsess them. Secrets don't stay secret for long, but they don't have to. Everything changes fast in the speed world.

Because it is a sport of old lineage and trades passed from one generation to the next, sons follow fathers and brothers follow one another. Among the dozens of multi-colored cars spilling onto the speedway for the first Winston Cup practice of the 1996 season, two were piloted by Bodines. For Brett Bodine, the baby-faced, thirty-seven-year-old middle brother of the upstate New York racing clan, it was more than the start of a new season. It was the start of a new life. Over the winter, he'd bought the last pieces of Junior Johnson's faded empire, allowing the white-haired legend to retire to the North Carolina mountains that made him famous. Every penny Brett had was riding on the gamble that he could make it on his own.

Feeling out the track, he veered down from the edge of the front stretch, taking an arc that resembled the flying patterns of the sea-gulls looping above the grandstands, until he was inside the first turn. It rose over him like an asphalt tidal wave, but to keep from getting lost in it, Brett stayed low, waiting for the mouth of the backstretch to appear so he could go throttle-down. When it's for real, it's called going WFO: *wide fuckin' open.* But this was just practice, so he dove back up and eased into the backstretch, letting it disappear beneath him at a calm 170 mph.

Then, quite suddenly and unexpectedly, Brett felt his legs beginning to bake. His heart tightened when he saw the source: flames snaking out from under the engine. Racers can walk away from catapulting crashes, but if there's one thing that scares them to death, it's fire. It's the one thing they can't outrun. Going into the fourth turn, he leaned hard into the brake, but it did no good because the flames had burned through the lines.

"I got a fire, I got a fire," he radioed, measuring his panic as the flames, being fed by the speed, began eating through the floorboard. He needed time to think, a way to get the car stopped. That's when he reached for the red lever by the driver's seat and sent fire-retardant dust spraying through the cockpit.

Coughing and blinded and still traveling at three times the normal speed limit, Brett threw his Ford into reverse in the hope it might lock the brakes, but nothing happened. That's when he realized he'd have to crash the damn thing to stop it. Bracing for the impact, he rammed the wheel right and scraped the outside wall. The impact threw his head back, but he held on tight, screeching along until he could spin himself into the grassy infield—almost precisely in front of a fire truck.

With flames pouring from beneath the car, he unbuckled his harness and unhooked the black cloth mesh covering his window, staggering out gasping for air and dizzy, but otherwise unharmed. As he was ushered into an ambulance, he looked back at the car that represented every waking hour of his effort for two months and thought, This can't be happening.

By the time he returned to his hauler, Brett's crew was already unloading the backup car that was parked on a lift in the elevated bay of their eighteen-wheeler. It was the car that no one hoped would be needed, the ugly sister. His crew unwrapped it and put on the track, but its speeds lagged. They tried one engine, then another, and when the clock ticked down on the weekend's practices without improvement, Brett made a desperation visit to a team known for its high-performance motors, and paid

$30,000 to lease one of their surplus engines for qualifying day. Even that didn't help. When his time came to go wide-open for real, he circled the oval at 185.835 mph, just thirty-sixth fastest of fifty-one cars.

In NASCAR, racers line up in two columns to take the green flag. Given the choice of lining up inside or outside, you want to be inside since the interior car has to travel less distance, and therefore has the advantage in a passing skirmish. The fastest car on qualifying day wins the right to line up in the first position on the inside row, also called the pole position, making that driver the pole-sitter. The second-fastest racer lines up in the first position on the outside row, the third-fastest qualifier gets the second position on the inside row, and so on, until a forty-two-car field is set in twenty-one rows.

The only exception to this system, the only one in a long season, is the Daytona 500. In Daytona the two fastest qualifiers get the first two positions, inside and outside the front row. But NASCAR fills the next fourteen rows by holding a unique pair of qualifying races on the Thursday before the 500. After a week of running practice laps alone, this prerace race gives drivers their first taste of close-contact battle, as well as a feel for how their car works in the often treacherous air currents of heavy traffic. Just as important, fans who've waited a long winter for a new season of racing get a thrilling prologue, and a preliminary look at whether their favorite driver will be strong on Sunday.

After the checkered flags fall on both of Thursday's races, known as the Gatorade Twin 125s because of their distance in miles, the top fourteen finishers in each are awarded spots in the second through fifteenth rows of Sunday's starting grid. With thirty drivers now selected, NASCAR officials populate the sixteenth through nineteenth rows by reexamining the prior week's trial speeds and choosing the fastest eight racers not yet selected.

This leaves four positions. To fill them, NASCAR gives out wild-card berths, known as "provisionals." A provisional is a free pass into the race, but to claim it you must have finished the prior season better than the next racer vying for it. If the four provisionals are doled out, and somehow there is an ex–Winston Cup champion who still hasn't made the cut, a forty-third position is created for him. This freebie is called, not surprisingly, the champion's provisional. If no ex-champion needs it, the slot is not filled, and only forty-two cars start the race.

Looking at his time flash over the computer, 185.835, Brett heaved a long sigh. It wasn't fatal. Though he'd never won a championship, he ended 1995 in twentieth place. The odds were that of the nineteen racers who finished the '95 season better, four would not need to use a provisional to get into Sunday's race. In other words, Brett's '95 finish was good enough that he'd be at the front of the line, or close to it, when NASCAR started doling them out.

But Brett also understood NASCAR wouldn't let him use an unlimited number of provisionals through the year. In fact, Winston Cup teams get only eight. If Brett could avoid it, he didn't want to waste one on the first race of the season. So he slept fitfully Wednesday night, realizing he had to perform well in the qualifying race. Thursday morning Brett said a small prayer as he slid through the window of the ugly sister, which, because of its poor time-trial speed, was assigned the second-to-last starting spot in his Gatorade 125.

In the early stages of the race, Brett worked the track like a chessboard, weaving his way to eighteenth place, and was about to march up farther when rain clouds burst, prompting race officials, worried about the slickened track, to order the yellow caution flag be waved from the stand above the start/finish line. After the flag drops, everyone must race back to the stripe to ensure their place, but once they pass it, the field is frozen as the pace car pulls in front of the leader. In this case, the top fourteen drivers stayed on the track, protecting their positions, but the rest of the pack turned onto pit road as they came upon the exit lane off the front stretch, grateful for the chance to improve their cars without losing too much position as the leaders circled the track at a crawl.

Brett knew that new tires would make him faster, but this was the maiden pit stop for his newly hired crew. Since the slightest glitch on pit road can kill the painstaking gains a driver makes on the track, Brett hoped for the best when he saw the "11" sign dangling on a pole over the pit wall. It was the mark his team used to tell him where to stop, and as he brought his Ford to a screeching halt, he immediately felt his jack man heave up its left side. At that, the two tire changers went to work, drilling loose the ten lug nuts securing his left-side tires and heaving the old shorn Goodyears off the wheels. The sweating, nervous front changer grabbed a fresh tire, mounted it, and with a move he'd practiced all winter, reached for his air gun to tighten the five lug nuts.

Except he forgot to switch the air gun off reverse. Instead of fastening them, it loosened them. In the precious seconds it took to reset the gun, Brett's rivals revved past him. When his crew chief yelled "Go! Go! Go!" Brett had lost so much time that he had nowhere to go but last place again.

But race cars have their own personalities, choosing when they want to kick in, and with ten laps to go, the ugly sister started handling beautifully, hugging the line in the turns, holding the draft in the straights. As Brett came within inches of a black Ford, he heard his crew chief say, "The number seven ahead is the cutoff."

"Ten-four," he radioed back. He knew he had to overtake car number 7 to get one of the fourteen transfer spots into Sunday's race. What he didn't acknowledge to his crew chief was the fact that his older brother Geoff was behind its wheel.

Sweeping inside, Brett took the position away from Geoff. But below him on the track another driver was breathing hard. With the front stretch disappearing under them, Bobby Hillin Jr. ducked out of the draft just long enough to power beneath Brett. But there was so little space between Brett and the car ahead that as Hillin tried wedging back into the draft, he nicked the ugly sister's nose, sending it straight into the wall. Brett's crew raced to their pit-side television in time to see him spinning down the infield and sliding into the Chevy driven by Bobby Labonte. The Chevrolet toppled onto its roof.

Brett finished the race in last place. As a result, he was beside himself as he sweated out the second of the day's races, praying his time-trial speed would still lift him into the race. But when the final tally was done, Brett had been beaten out by his brother. The pair, separated by ten years, barely spoke to each other, the result of rifts that had to do with racing and family, but the divide that mattered most to Brett was the six-tenths of a second that Geoff had over him in the time trials. It meant that for his first race as an owner, Brett would need to use a provisional. And all he had left to show for his trouble were two totaled cars.

With four days to go, five bleary-eyed mechanics in Mooresville, North Carolina, were in the midst of a round-the-clock vigil to repair the first wreck. They fixed the front snout, reconstructed the body and repainted it. Then they trucked it to Daytona late Thursday, worked on it in the garage, and when the track closed for the day, stayed up in their hotel parking lot building a fuel cell and exhaust system. Practicing with it on Saturday, February 17, Brett was amazed to find it actually ran faster than before.

Calling his frazzled team together in his trailer that afternoon, he was dizzy from having pulled off the nearly impossible.

"We haven't lost any points," he said. "We're in the same square as Dale Earnhardt and Jeff Gordon. Rusty Wallace is starting behind us. Hey, we're still in this thing."

Hard as it might have seemed to believe, it was true.

The first race of the season hadn't even begun yet.

*Also available from
Ballantine Books:*

KEEPIN' IT COUNTRY
The George Strait Story

by

Jo Sgammato

Keepin' It Country explores what America loves so much about George Strait: the tremendous talent he generously shares while keeping his own life private, his authentic country life and spirit, and his renown as a true gentleman whose career is the bridge between the past and the future of country music.

KEEPIN' IT COUNTRY
The George Strait Story
by Jo Sgammato

Published by Ballantine Books.
Available in bookstores everywhere.

The dazzling rise of a young country star . . .

DREAM COME TRUE
The LeAnn Rimes Story
by Jo Sgammato

LeAnn Rimes, owner of a huge, God-given voice, was born knowing what she wanted to do and sang with assurance when she was just a toddler. She burst onto the country-music scene with one great song, "Blue," an old-fashioned ballad originally written for the legendary Patsy Cline. Her album of the same name hit the charts at number one, and LeAnn became one of the biggest entertainment stories of the year.

But as young as she was, this overnight sensation was years in the making. Here is the heartwarming story of LeAnn Rimes and her parents, Belinda and Wilbur Rimes, an American family who made a DREAM COME TRUE.

Published by Ballantine Books.
Available wherever books are sold.

*Lorrie Morgan was born to be
a country-western music star.*

In FOREVER YOURS, FAITHFULLY,
she tells her tempestuous story of sweet
triumph and bitter tragedy.
From her childhood as a Nashville blueblood,
performing at the Grand Ole Opry at the tender
age of eleven, to her turbulent,
star-crossed love affair with Keith Whitley,
a bluegrass legend she loved passionately
but could not save from his personal demons,
to her rise to superstardom,
she lays bare all the secrets and great passions
of a life lived to the fullest.

And her story would not be complete without
the music that has been her lifeline.

**A special four-song CD of
never-before-released material,
featuring a duet with Keith Whitley,
is included with this hardcover.**

FOREVER YOURS, FAITHFULLY
by Lorrie Morgan

Published by Ballantine Books.
Available wherever books are sold.